TAKS STUDY GUIDE

Texas Assessment of Knowledge and Skills

D1609353

Grade 10

English Language Arts

A Student and Family Guide

Contents

English Language Arts

Introduction 9

Sample Reading Selections 11

Objective 1: Basic Understanding 24

  What Is a Basic Understanding? 24

  Reading in Varied Sources 26

  Why Develop Good Reading Skills? 26

  What Are Some Strategies for Reading? 27

  Understanding Word Meanings 29

  Summarizing 33

  Identifying Supporting Details 35

Objective 2: Literary Elements and Techniques 37

  Analyzing Setting 38

  Analyzing Characters 39

  Describing and Analyzing Plot, Conflict, and Resolution 40

  Recognizing Theme 42

  Using Text to Defend Responses 43

  Understanding Literary Language 44

  Connecting Literature to Historical Context 45

  Understanding Literary Terms 46

Objective 3: Analysis and Critical Evaluation 48

  Analyzing Text Structures 49

  Making Inferences, Drawing Conclusions,
  and Making Predictions 50

  Analyzing Across Texts 52

  Identifying Author's Purpose 52

  Author's Craft 54

Contents

English Language Arts (continued)

Credibility of Information Sources 55

Modes of Persuasion 56

Understanding Ideas and Relationships in Media 57

Understanding the Purpose of Media 59

Finding the Main Point of a Media Message 61

Recognizing Persuasion in Media 62

Short-Answer Items 64

On Your Own 71

Reading Answer Key 78

Objectives 4 and 5: Written Composition 81

What Are the Writing Prompts Like? 81

How Will My Composition Be Scored? 82

Sample Compositions 84

The Writing Process 89

Prewriting 90

Composing 91

Revising 92

Editing 93

Publishing 94

On Your Own 95

Objective 6: Revising and Editing 102

Organization 102

Supporting Sentences 102

Sequence/Progression 104

Transitions 106

Contents

English Language Arts (continued)

Sentence Structure. 107

Complete Sentences 107

Sentence Fragments 107

Run-on Sentences. 108

Awkward Sentences 110

Misplaced Modifiers 110

Avoiding Redundancy 111

Combining Sentences 112

Standard English Usage 116

Subject-Verb Agreement 116

Verb Tense 118

Pronoun-Antecedent Agreement 120

Pronoun Case. 121

Clear Pronoun Reference 123

Double Indicators 124

Correct Word Choice. 124

Informal Language 125

Confusing Parts of Speech 125

Adjectives Versus Adverbs. 126

Mechanics 127

Punctuation 127

Capitalization 131

Spelling 132

Contents

English Language Arts (continued)

Using the Skills **133**

    Revising and Editing a Paper **133**

    **How Does TAKS Test the Skills You Have
Been Reviewing?** **140**

    On Your Own: Practice Passage 1 and Questions **141**

    On Your Own: Practice Passage 2 and Questions **145**

Revising and Editing Answer Key **149**

ENGLISH LANGUAGE ARTS

INTRODUCTION

What Is This Book?

This is a study guide to help you strengthen your skills on the Grade 10 TAKS English Language Arts (ELA) test.

©Jose Luis Pelaez, Inc./CORBIS

How Is the Grade 10 TAKS English Language Arts Test Organized?

The TAKS ELA test combines reading and writing skills. One section of the test addresses reading and written composition skills, and another section addresses revising and editing skills. The ELA test measures achievement of certain test objectives, or goals. The TAKS objectives are broad statements about the knowledge or skills being tested. You can find out more about the reading and writing objectives for Grade 10 beginning on page 24 of this book. Here's an example of a TAKS objective for Grade 10 reading:

The student will demonstrate an understanding of the effects of literary elements and techniques in culturally diverse written texts.

What does this mean? It means that students should be able to show that they understand how certain elements of a story—such as **conflict** and **literary language**—affect the story's meaning. The phrase "culturally diverse" means "having to do with a wide range of backgrounds and points of view."

There are three types of questions on the TAKS ELA test: multiple-choice items, short-answer items, and a writing prompt.

- In a **multiple-choice** item, you choose the correct answer from four possible answers.

- In a **short-answer** item, you write a brief response to a question.

- For a **writing prompt**, you write a composition on an assigned topic.

What Is a Triplet?

At Grade 10 the reading portion of the TAKS ELA test contains three selections. The three selections are related; this is why they are called a triplet.

A common theme or idea links all the selections in the triplet. These selections are carefully chosen to reflect a variety of backgrounds, experiences, and points of view. They are much like the selections you read in the classroom and in your everyday life.

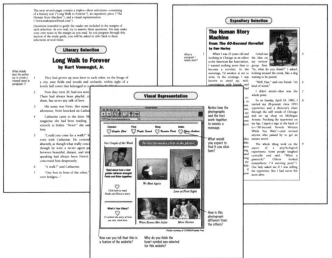

Each triplet consists of

- a published literary selection (such as a short story or a chapter from a novel)

- a published expository, or informational, selection (such as an essay or a magazine article)

- a one-page viewing and representing piece (such as an advertisement, a Web page, or a cartoon)

How Can This Study Guide Help You?

This study guide can help you strengthen the skills tested on the TAKS test. It explains the objectives that are tested and guides you through sample questions. These questions give you practice in applying the skills you have learned in the classroom. When you work through this study guide, you'll be working on the same skills that you'll need to do well on the test.

How Is This Study Guide Organized?

This study guide begins by presenting a sample triplet.

- The first selection is a short story.

- The second selection is an essay.

- The third selection is a Web page.

You will see notes in the margins of each selection. These notes will highlight important points that careful readers notice as they read.

Next the study guide gives you information about TAKS Objectives 1 through 6. Objectives 1 through 3 are reading objectives, Objectives 4 and 5 deal with the written composition, and Objective 6 covers revising and editing skills. Along with this information, you'll find sample

items. These items show you how TAKS tests the skills in these objectives. The sample questions in the study guide are the same types of questions as those on the TAKS test and are at about the same level of difficulty.

This study guide contains answers to all the sample TAKS questions. Some of the answers appear in the sections that focus on the objectives, and others are found at the end of each section. The answers include explanations that tell why an answer is correct or incorrect.

The next several pages contain a triplet—three selections—consisting of a literary text ("Long Walk to Forever"), an expository piece ("The Human Story Machine"), and a visual representation ("www.makeanewfriend.com").

Questions intended to guide the reader are included in the margins of each selection. As you read, try to answer these questions. You may make your own notes in the margins as you read. As you progress through the reading section of this study guide, you will be asked to refer to these selections several times.

Literary Selection

Long Walk to Forever
by Kurt Vonnegut, Jr.

What details does the author use to create a tranquil mood in paragraph 1?

1   They had grown up next door to each other, on the fringe of a city, near fields and woods and orchards, within sight of a lovely bell tower that belonged to a school for the blind.

2   Now they were 20, had not seen each other for nearly a year. There had always been playful, comfortable warmth between them, but never any talk of love.

3   His name was Newt. Her name was Catharine. In the early afternoon, Newt knocked on Catharine's front door.

4   Catharine came to the door. She was carrying a fat, glossy magazine she had been reading. The magazine was devoted entirely to brides. "Newt!" she said. She was surprised to see him.

5   "Could you come for a walk?" he said. He was a shy person, even with Catharine. He covered his shyness by speaking absently, as though what really concerned him were far away—as though he were a secret agent pausing briefly on a mission between beautiful, distant, and sinister points. This manner of speaking had always been Newt's style, even in matters that concerned him desperately.

6   "A walk?" said Catharine.

7   "One foot in front of the other," said Newt, "through leaves, over bridges—"

8   "I had no idea you were in town," she said.

9   "Just this minute got in," he said.

10   "Still in the Army, I see," she said.

What details does the author use to characterize Newt in paragraph 11? What can you infer about Newt from these details?

11   "Seven more months to go," he said. He was a private first class in the Artillery. His uniform was rumpled. His shoes were dusty. He needed a shave. He held out his hand for the magazine. "Let's see the pretty book," he said.

12   She gave it to him. "I'm getting married, Newt," she said.

13   "I know," he said. "Let's go for a walk."

14   "I'm awfully busy, Newt," she said. "The wedding is only a week away."

15   "If we go for a walk," he said, "it will make you rosy. It will make you a rosy bride." He turned the pages of the magazine. "A rosy bride like her—like her—like her," he said, showing her rosy brides.

What does Newt invite Catharine to do?

16   Catharine turned rosy, thinking about rosy brides.

17   "That will be my present to Henry Stewart Chasens," said Newt. "By taking you for a walk, I'll be giving him a rosy bride."

18   "You know his name?" said Catharine.

19   "Mother wrote," he said. "From Pittsburgh?"

20   "Yes," she said. "You'd like him."

21   "Maybe," he said.

22   "Can—can you come to the wedding, Newt?" she said.

23   "That I doubt," he said.

24   "Your furlough isn't for long enough?" she said.

25   "Furlough?" said Newt. He was studying a two-page ad for flat silver. "I'm not on furlough," he said.

26   "Oh?" she said.

27   "I'm what they call A.W.O.L.,"[1] said Newt.

What is Catharine's reaction when she learns that Newt is A.W.O.L.?

28   "Oh, Newt! You're not!" she said.

29   "Sure I am," he said, still looking at the magazine.

[1]A.W.O.L. is a military term for "absent without leave."

30   "Why, Newt?" she said.

What is ironic about this statement?

31   "I had to find out what your silver pattern is," he said. He read names of silver patterns from the magazine. "Albermarle? Heather?" he said. "Legend? Rambler Rose?" He looked up, smiled. "I plan to give you and your husband a spoon," he said.

What details lead you to believe that Newt does not really want to buy Catharine and Henry a spoon?

32   "Newt, Newt—tell me really," she said.

33   "I want to go for a walk," he said.

34   She wrung her hands in sisterly anguish. "Oh, Newt—you're fooling me about being A.W.O.L.," she said.

35   Newt imitated a police siren softly, raised his eyebrows.

36   "Where—where from?" she said.

37   "Fort Bragg," he said.

38   "North Carolina?" she said.

39   "That's right," he said. "Near Fayetteville—where Scarlet O'Hara went to school."

40   "How did you get here, Newt?" she said.

41   He raised his thumb, jerked it in a hitchhike gesture. "Two days," he said.

Newt says that he did not come to see his mother. What can you infer from this?

42   "Does your mother know?" she said.

43   "I didn't come to see my mother," he told her.

44   "Who did you come to see?" she said.

45   "You," he said.

46   "Why me?" she said.

Why do you think Newt repeats this phrase from paragraph 7?

47   "Because I love you," he said. "Now can we take a walk?" he said. "One foot in front of the other—through leaves, over bridges—"

Why do you think the author includes an extra space here?

48   They were taking the walk now, were in a woods with a brown-leaf floor.

49   Catharine was angry and rattled, close to tears. "Newt," she said, "this is absolutely crazy."

50   "How so?" said Newt.

Catharine says that she agreed to go for a walk with Newt to get him out of the house. Do you think that this is her real reason?

How would you summarize Catharine's "speech"? What characteristics does it reveal about her?

What conflict does Catharine's speech reveal?

How does the author reveal Catharine's affection for Newt in paragraph 61?

51   "What a crazy time to tell me you love me," she said. "You never talked that way before." She stopped walking.

52   "Let's keep walking," he said.

53   "No," she said. "So far, no farther. I shouldn't have come out with you at all," she said.

54   "You did," he said.

55   "To get you out of the house," she said. "If somebody walked in and heard you talking to me that way, a week before the wedding—"

56   "What would they think?" he said.

57   "They'd think you were crazy," she said.

58   "Why?" he said.

59   Catharine took a deep breath, made a speech. "Let me say that I'm deeply honored by this crazy thing you've done," she said. "I can't believe you're really A.W.O.L., but maybe you are. I can't believe you really love me, but maybe you do. But—"

60   "I do," said Newt.

61   "Well, I'm deeply honored," said Catharine, "and I'm very fond of you as a friend, Newt, extremely fond—but it's just too late." She took a step away from him. "You've never even kissed me," she said, and she protected herself with her hands. "I don't mean you should do it now. I just mean this is all so unexpected. I haven't got the remotest idea of how to respond."

62   "Just walk some more," he said. "Have a nice time."

63   They started walking again.

64   "How did you expect me to react?" she said.

65   "How would I know what to expect?" he said. "I've never done anything like this before."

66   "Did you think I would throw myself into your arms?" she said.

67   "Maybe," he said.

68   "I'm sorry to disappoint you," she said.

69   "I'm not disappointed," he said. "I wasn't counting on it. This is very nice, just walking."

70   Catharine stopped again. "You know what happens next?" she said.

71   "Nope," he said.

72   "We shake hands," she said. "We shake hands and part friends," she said. "That's what happens next."

How would you describe Newt's approach to pursuing Catharine? What does this show about him?

73   Newt nodded. "All right," he said. "Remember me from time to time. Remember how much I loved you."

74   Involuntarily, Catharine burst into tears. She turned her back to Newt, looked into the infinite colonnade of the woods.

75   "What does that mean?" said Newt.

76   "Rage!" said Catharine. She clenched her hands. "You have no right—"

Catharine feels that her tears are caused by rage. What other emotions might be causing her outburst?

77   "I had to find out," he said.

78   "If I'd loved you," she said, "I would have let you know before now."

79   "You would?" he said.

80   "Yes," she said. She faced him, looked up at him, her face quite red. "You would have known," she said.

81   "How?" he said.

82   "You would have seen it," she said. "Women aren't very clever at hiding it."

Notice the context clues for the word consternation.

83   Newt looked closely at Catharine's face now. To her consternation, she realized that what she had said was true, that a woman couldn't hide love.

84   Newt was seeing love now.

85   And he did what he had to do. He kissed her.

86   "You're hell to get along with!" she said when Newt let her go.

87   "I am?" said Newt.

88   "You shouldn't have done that," she said.

89   "You didn't like it?" he said.

90   "What did you expect," she said—"wild, abandoned passion?"

91   "I keep telling you," he said, "I never know what's going to happen next."

92   "We say good-bye," she said.

93   He frowned slightly. "All right," he said.

94   She made another speech. "I'm not sorry we kissed," she said. "That was sweet. We should have kissed, we've been so close. I'll always remember you, Newt, and good luck."

What important change does the author reveal to the reader?

95   "You too," he said.

96   "Thank you, Newt," she said.

97   "Thirty days," he said.

98   "What?" she said.

99   "Thirty days in the stockade," he said—"that's what one kiss will cost me."

100   "I—I'm sorry," she said, "but I didn't ask you to go A.W.O.L."

101   "I know," he said.

102   "You certainly don't deserve any hero's reward for doing something as foolish as that," she said.

103   "Must be nice to be a hero," said Newt. "Is Henry Stewart Chasens a hero?"

What can you infer from the fact that Catharine continues to walk?

104   "He might be, if he got the chance," said Catharine. She noted uneasily that they had begun to walk again. The farewell had been forgotten.

105   "You really love him?" he said.

106   "Certainly I love him!" she said hotly. "I wouldn't marry him if I didn't love him!"

107   "What's good about him?" said Newt.

108   "Honestly!" she cried, stopping again. "Do you have an idea how offensive you're being? Many, many, many things are good about Henry! Yes," she said, "and many, many, many things are probably bad too. But that isn't any of your business. I love Henry, and I don't have to argue his merits with you!"

How would you describe Catharine's feelings toward Henry?

109   "Sorry," said Newt.

110   "Honestly!" said Catharine.

111   Newt kissed her again. He kissed her again because she wanted him to.

112   They were now in a large orchard.

113   "How did we get so far from home, Newt?" said Catharine.

114   "One foot in front of the other—through leaves, over bridges," said Newt.

115   "They add up—the steps," she said.

116   Bells rang in the tower of the school for the blind nearby.

117   "School for the blind," said Newt.

118   "School for the blind," said Catharine. She shook her head in drowsy wonder. "I've got to go back now," she said.

119   "Say good-bye," said Newt.

120   "Every time I do," said Catharine, "I seem to get kissed."

121   Newt sat down on the close-cropped grass under an apple tree. "Sit down," he said.

122   "No," she said.

123   "I won't touch you," he said.

124   "I don't believe you," she said.

125   She sat down under another tree, 20 feet away from him. She closed her eyes.

Why do you think Newt tells Catharine to dream of Henry?

126   "Dream of Henry Stewart Chasens," he said.

127   "What?" she said.

128   "Dream of your wonderful husband-to-be," he said.

129   "All right, I will," she said. She closed her eyes tighter, caught glimpses of her husband-to-be.

130   Newt yawned.

131   The bees were humming in the trees, and Catharine almost fell asleep. When she opened her eyes she saw that Newt really was asleep.

132   He began to snore softly.

133   Catharine let Newt sleep for an hour, and while he slept she adored him with all her heart.

134   The shadows of the apple tree grew to the east. The bells in the tower of the school for the blind rang again.

135   "Chick-a-dee-dee-dee," went a chickadee.

136   Somewhere far away an automobile starter nagged and failed, nagged and failed, fell still.

What are paragraphs 132–137 mostly about?

137   Catharine came out from under her tree, knelt by Newt.

138   "Newt?" she said.

139   "H'm?" he said. He opened his eyes.

140   "Late," she said.

141   "Hello, Catharine," he said.

142   "Hello, Newt," she said.

143   "I love you," he said.

144   "I know," she said.

145   "Too late," he said.

146   "Too late," she said.

147   He stood, stretched groaningly. "A very nice walk," he said.

148   "I thought so," she said.

149   "Part company here?" he said.

150   "Where will you go?" she said.

151   "Hitch into town, turn myself in," he said.

152   "Good luck," she said.

What characteristic of Newt does paragraph 153 reveal?

153   "You, too," he said. "Marry me, Catharine?"

154   "No," she said.

155   He smiled, stared at her hard for a moment, then walked away quickly.

156   Catharine watched him grow smaller in the long perspective of shadows and trees, knew that if he stopped and turned now, if he called to her, she would run to him. She would have no choice.

Why does the author use short sentences in paragraph 157?

157   Newt did stop. He did turn. He did call. "Catharine," he called.

158   She ran to him, put her arms around him, could not speak.

The Human Story Machine
from *The 60-Second Novelist*
by Dan Hurley

© Greg Vimont 2002

What is paragraph 1 mainly about?

1   When I was 25 years old and working in Chicago as an editor at the American Bar Association, I wanted nothing more than to become a novelist. In the mornings, I'd awaken at six to write. In the evenings, I was known to stand up, mid-conversation with friends, and announce I had an idea and had to go home to write.

What does Hurley's costume idea show about him?

2   One October day, a co-worker and I were trying to think up Halloween costumes. "How about if I went as a writer, with a typewriter slung from my shoulders?" I asked. "I could walk around like one of those cigarette girls, saying, 'Short stories? Novels?'"

3   Of course, I never did it.

What do you think Hurley means by "performance writing"?

4   But something about the idea grabbed me: writing in public on demand; not performance art, but performance writing. Behind the absurdity, I sensed the possibility of touching people more directly with my writing than I ever had while sitting alone at my desk. If nothing else, it would be a great story for my grandchildren.

5   I tried out the idea on my writers' group first. "So, what do you think?" I asked, looking around the room, like a dog waiting to be petted.

6   "Well, Dan," said one friend, "it's kind of weird."

7   I didn't mind—that was the whole point.

8   So on Sunday, April 24, 1983, I carried my 28-pound, circa 1953 typewriter and a director's chair through the stiff winds of Chicago and set up shop on Michigan Avenue. Perching the typewriter on my lap, I taped a sign to the back of it—"60-Second Novels Written While You Wait"—and invited anyone who passed by to get an instant novel.

9   The whole thing took on the aspect of a psychological experiment. Some people laughed cynically and said, "What a gimmick!" Others looked sympathetic ("A starving poet!"). One lady asked me if I was selling the typewriter. But I had never felt more alive.

Where does Hurley get his idea for the title for his first instant novel?

How would you describe the interaction between Hurley and the crowd? What details does Hurley use to show this?

What are paragraphs 13 and 14 mostly about?

What words in paragraph 16 are clues to the meaning of venue?

10   Then a couple walked up. "I don't know what you're doing," the woman said, "but whatever it is, I want one." The man added, with a wry smile, "It certainly is something extremely unusual."

11   I asked their names (plus a few other nosy questions) and began writing. I titled their story, "Something Extremely Unusual."

12   As I typed, I noticed shoes crowding toward me on the sidewalk. Whispers and chuckles came from behind my back. When I finally pulled the page out of the typewriter, I looked up to see about 25 people surrounding me.

13   "Read it!" shouted a few of them. I did. And when it was over, they applauded. In that moment, the entire direction of my life veered off-road. I had no idea what I had discovered—or what had discovered me—but I could see that it worked. So I wrote another, and another. Rather than scaring me into silence, the crowd spurred me on. They were the ultimate deadline.

14   My life took on a Clark Kent–Superman split: mild-mannered reporter for the ABA by day; 60-Second Novelist, fighting a battle for literature and tips, by night.

15   That first summer, I feared I was turning into a Stupid Human Trick: "Dan Hurley, the human story machine. Put in a word, he spits out a story!" I also feared that I'd soon get bored. But 17 years and thousands of novels later, I'm still waiting.

16   I've since devoted my life to writing these novels: on streets and online, at department stores and trade shows, at bars and bar mitzvahs. No venue is too ordinary or bizarre.

17   The longer I keep at it, the more people seem to open up to me. They give me their trust. I give them stories that are some hitherto unknown confection of fact, fiction, fable and bibliotherapy. But before I type the first word, I give them something else: my ears, my eyes, my total, 200-percent attention.

18   At this point, there aren't enough seats in Madison Square Garden to contain all the people I've written for (by now the figure is more than 25,000). From the first day, I kept a carbon copy of each story. The pile of tissue-thin duplicates now stands over four feet tall in my study. They're white, green, pink, blue and yellow—a rainbow of stories, a pillar of life's little lessons.

19   There may be no getting around the Stupid Human Trick aspect of it all. But I'd like to think there's something more, something that speaks to the incredible power of the

life stories we tell about ourselves. After all, everyone's a born author of his or her own life story.

20 Here is my favorite.

21 At a seaside amusement park north of New York City, I wrote this story for a pretty young woman named Alice, in which I dared to predict her future:

22 "A Walk Along the Ocean"

23 Alice went out with a guy for four years and then he broke up with her because he was confused, which made her very unhappy at the time, but now she thinks it was for the best. In the year and a half since then, she has gone out on dates, but either she likes the guy and he doesn't like her, or vice versa.

24 Well, this is all pretty rotten.

25 So she has taken to seeing her grandmother, a very wise woman, encouraging and loving. Alice talks with her and feels much better, and finds warmth and laughter. But how will she ever find true love?

26 One day, after visiting her grandmother, Alice will go for a walk along the ocean, and she shall meet a man. He will ask her a question and the first thing she will think is, "Wow, is this guy *something*!" and they will talk and fall in love.

27 He might come from a ship. He might be swimming. He might be walking. Maybe he will fall from the sky, or maybe he will come from beneath the waves. But the important thing is he will come from the ocean after she goes to see her Grandma and isn't even thinking about a man. For there are plenty of fish in the sea, and many men, too.

28 The fact that Alice and I met not 20 yards from the water's edge didn't occur to me the day I wrote her story. Two months later I walked into a writing class and sat down in the only available seat. "Remember me?" said the person beside me. It was Alice.

29 We've been married for nine years now and have a beautiful five-year-old daughter, Anne. We're living proof that you can rewrite your life story to find a happy ending.

30 And so, not only did my crazy idea to write stories on the street bring me a career, it brought me a wife and a family. I guess you could say my dream of becoming a novelist also came true. Not quite the way I had anticipated—writing novels on the street, one page in length, one person at a time. But then, no good story turns out the way you expect.

Dan Hurley writes 60-second novels at www.instantnovelist.com.

Do you agree that people's life stories hold a certain power?

How would you summarize "A Walk Along the Ocean"?

Visual Representation

Internet Browser

File   Edit   View   Go   Help

Back   Forward   Reload   Home   Search   Stop   Print

Location   http://www.makeanewfriend.com

Connect   Find   Shop   Index
♡ *Couples Chat*   ♡ *People Search*   ♡ *Vacation Deals*   ♡ *Story Archives*

Our Couple of the Week

To view the stories, click on the photos.

Read about how a lost golden retriever brought Paula and Brian together.

♡

Click here to read Paula and Brian's story.

What's Your Story?

♡

To submit the story of how you met, click here.

We Meet Again

Love at First Sight

When Romeo Met Juliet

More Stories

Photos courtesy of CORBIS/Royalty Free.

Notice how the photographs and the text work together to convey a message.

What would you expect to find if you click here?

How is this photograph different from the others?

How can you tell that this is a feature of the website?

Why do you think the heart symbol was selected for this Web page?

Objective 1

The student will demonstrate a basic understanding of culturally diverse written texts.

The TAKS ELA test is based on the student expectations in the Texas Essential Knowledge and Skills (TEKS) curriculum; this curriculum is what you are being taught every day at school. The student expectations for Objective 1 tell what students should be able to do as they read to understand the basic meaning of a selection.

What Is a Basic Understanding?

Having a **basic understanding** of what you read means much more than just seeing what is on the printed page. It means being able to

- read and understand many different types of texts
- find the meanings of words you read by using context clues and other ways of figuring out word meanings

I can tell from this sentence that *inequitable* means "not fair."

• recognize important details in a selection

• understand the "big picture"—that is, what a selection is mainly about

The skills above are "building block" skills. They are the skills that you need in order to develop a deeper understanding of what you read.

Reading in Varied Sources

You will find that the reading selections for the TAKS test are very much like the materials you read every day. For example, you might be asked to read a magazine article about a group of teenagers performing community service. Or you might read a novel excerpt about a woman who stands up for her beliefs. Perhaps you'll be required to read and interpret an advertisement for a sporting-goods store.

Why Develop Good Reading Skills?

Being able to read effectively is extremely important both in and out of school. As you move from grade to grade, reading skills are necessary for academic success in all subjects. In your life outside school, reading skills are crucial to developing a deeper understanding of the world around you. Good readers live in a wider, richer world. There are more opportunities available to good readers throughout their lives—in education beyond high school, in jobs, and in personal growth.

©Photodisc

In high school you are learning to explore text at deeper levels of understanding. You are analyzing how literary elements in text reveal meaning. You're also learning how an author crafts a piece of writing to affect the way readers read and understand the writing. And perhaps most importantly, you're learning how to make connections between what you read and what you already know. In other words, you're not just becoming a better reader; you're becoming a better thinker.

What Are Some Strategies for Reading?

To understand what you read requires becoming an **active reader**. Active reading involves using several skills to get meaning from text.

Before you read

Before you read a selection from beginning to end, it's helpful to get a general idea of what the selection is about. You might briefly look through the selection—read the title, look at the pictures, remember what you already know about the topic, and notice how the selection is organized.

Begin asking questions about the selection. Here's a chart that you can use before, during, and after reading:

What I Already Know	What I Want to Know	What I Have Learned

As you read

As you read a selection, continue to ask yourself questions:

- **What is the tone of this paragraph?**
- **How is the setting important?**
- **How would I summarize this article?**

Look at the questions in the margins of the reading selections on pages 11–23. These are the types of questions that careful readers ask themselves as they read. They're also the same types of questions you might find on the TAKS test.

Charts or other visual organizers can help you keep track of information as you read. They can increase your understanding of a selection and organize your thoughts about it. Graphic organizers help you see relationships among ideas and information in a text. Venn diagrams, time lines, cause-and-effect charts, and story maps are examples of graphic organizers.

Here's an example of a graphic organizer for reading fiction, illustrated with a story you may have read in a textbook. You may have used **story maps** in your classroom reading. Story maps organize the important information in a story and track the sequence of events.

Title: "The First Seven Years" by Bernard Malamud

Main Characters: Feld, Miriam, Max, Sobel

Setting: 1949, Jewish immigrant community of Manhattan's Lower East Side

Conflict: A shoemaker's daughter does not care for the man her father wants her to marry.

Overall Theme: Devotion in love

Problem/Goal: A shoemaker dreams of a better life for his daughter.

Diagrams are an efficient way to organize ideas and can be useful for taking notes when reading nonfiction. They can help you retain information as you read in depth. For example, you might diagram a chapter in a science textbook, charting the topic or main idea as well as the subtopics or supporting details.

Here's an example of a diagram for reading nonfiction. This type of chart is a **tree diagram**, which lists the pros and cons of an argument. It summarizes part of a magazine article about school uniforms.

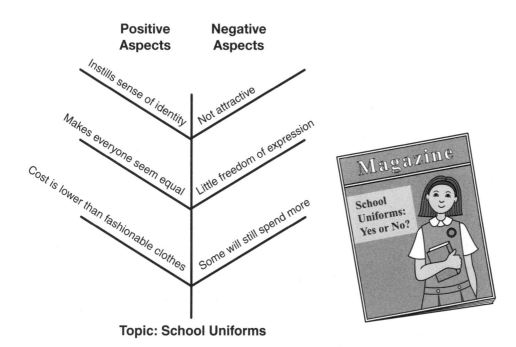

Understanding Word Meanings

On the TAKS ELA test, you will be asked to determine the meaning of certain words from the selections. One way to find the meaning of a word is to look it up in a dictionary. Another way is to look for clues in the selection. Often other words and sentences give you a good idea of a word's meaning. Knowing how to recognize these clues can help you figure out the meaning of unfamiliar words.

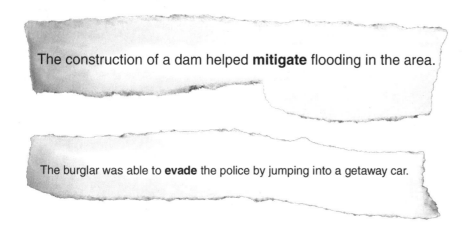

The construction of a dam helped **mitigate** flooding in the area.

The burglar was able to **evade** the police by jumping into a getaway car.

Using Context Clues

You can often figure out the meaning of an unfamiliar word by looking at context clues.

Context clues are details that clarify the meaning of a word. These clues are sometimes obvious and sometimes not so obvious. If you know what to look for, though, and read carefully, you can often figure out the meaning of an unfamiliar word.

Here are some examples of different types of context clues:

● **Definition**

> A distillate is a concentrated liquid.

The phrase "a concentrated liquid" defines *distillate*.

● **Figurative language**

> The beard on her grandfather's cheek felt as abrasive as sandpaper.

The figurative language "as abrasive as" tells you that the author is comparing a man's beard with sandpaper. This can help you figure out that *abrasive* means "rough."

● **Multiple-meaning words**

> The artist longed for fame but remained obscure her entire life.

The word *obscure* has four meanings: (1) not clearly expressed, (2) not well known, (3) hidden, and (4) not distinct. The phrase "longed for fame" coupled with "but" tells you that *obscure* in this sentence means "not well known."

Here's an example of the type of context question you might find on the TAKS ELA test. Return to "The Human Story Machine" on pages 20–22. Reread paragraph 16. Then answer the question below:

> In paragraph 16, the word *venue* means —
>
> A a chapter
>
> B a moment
>
> C a sequence
>
> D a location

Two context clues help you figure out that *venue* means "a location." The author lists a series of locations where he writes his novels in public: on streets, online, in department stores, and at bar mitzvahs. Then in the next sentence he gives the additional information that no *venue* is "too ordinary or bizarre."

When you are studying the possible answers to vocabulary questions, it is sometimes helpful to substitute each answer choice in the sentence to see whether it fits. In other words, if you substitute the word *location* in the sentence ("No location is too ordinary or bizarre"), you see that it makes sense. Answer Choices A, B, and C do not make sense.

TIP:
✔ This strategy does not work for every vocabulary question.

Using Prefixes, Roots, and Suffixes

Knowing the meanings of prefixes, roots, and suffixes can help you figure out the meanings of many unfamiliar words.

A **prefix** is a word part added before a root to change its meaning.

> *Sound* means "free from defect."
>
> The prefix *un-* means "not."
>
> *Unsound* means "not free from defect."

The **root** is the foundation on which a word is built. The root carries the word's core meaning, and it is the part to which prefixes and suffixes are added. In the example above, *sound* is the root of *unsound*.

A **suffix** is a word part added after a root to change its meaning.

> *Child* means "a young person."
>
> The suffix *-ish* means "like."
>
> *Childish* means "like a young person."

Using Glossaries and Dictionaries

While reading a selection, have you ever come to a word that seems to have a different meaning from the one you are used to seeing? This can make the entire selection confusing. As you read, watch for words that have **multiple meanings**, such as *tire, draft,* and *prize.*

To choose the correct meaning of a word, consider the word's part of speech and context. When you use a glossary or a dictionary, you can look up all the meanings of a word to discover which meaning fits the context in which the word is used.

Here's an example of the type of multiple-meaning question you might find on the TAKS ELA test. Return to "Long Walk to Forever" on pages 11–19. Reread paragraph 49. Then answer the question below.

Read the following dictionary entry.

> **rattle** \ˈra-t'l\ *verb* **1.** to make rapid sharp noises one after another **2.** to upset or embarrass to the point of loss of composure **3.** to move about in a large empty space **4.** to speak or perform in a brisk, lively manner

Which definition best matches the use of the word *rattled* in paragraph 49?

A Definition 1

B Definition 2

C Definition 3

D Definition 4

To find the correct answer, first reread paragraph 49 and notice that it is mostly about how Catharine responds to Newt's surprising declaration of love. Next consider how each definition would fit into the context of the paragraph. Then choose the meaning that makes the most sense in the sentence.

Choice A does not make sense because the sentence is not about a noise. Choice B does make sense because Catharine loses her composure when Newt tells her that he loves her. Some readers may be tempted to choose C because Newt and Catharine are taking a walk in the woods, a large space. However, careful readers will remember that the word *rattled* refers only to Catharine, not the woods. Choice D does not fit because the sentence is not about how Catharine speaks or performs.

Summarizing

A **summary** captures the main points of a story or other text, boiling it down to a few words or sentences. When you summarize, you use your own words to briefly state the main ideas and key details of the text. Reading a summary is one way to get a sense of the important points of a selection or book without reading the whole text. Writing a summary helps you understand the key ideas. When referring to fiction, such as novels or short stories, we use the term **plot summary** to describe the condensed version of what happens in the text.

Here's an example of the type of question you might find on the TAKS ELA test. Return to "Long Walk to Forever," on pages 11–19. Review the story. Then answer the question below.

"Long Walk to Forever" tells the story of —

A a young woman who is preparing for her wedding

B a young man who visits his hometown for the weekend

C a young couple who realize that they love each other

D a soldier who decides to run away from the army

Answer Choice C is the most complete overview of the story. Choices B and D contain important details, but these choices do not even mention Catharine, who is a major character in the story. Choice A offers background information from the story but does not mention Newt.

Looking at the "Big Picture"

The **gist** or main idea is the most important point a writer wants to make. A piece of writing can have an overall message, such as "Although Sandra misses Denver, she begins to appreciate the beauty of New Orleans."

Often a main point is easy to identify because it is clearly stated. It answers the question "What is this selection or excerpt about?" Stated main ideas are sometimes found in the first or last sentence of a paragraph. Read the paragraph below and identify what it is mainly about.

New Orleans has many tourist attractions. You may want to begin your visit by dropping by the aquarium, located near the Mississippi River. Afterward, wander through the French Quarter, an old section of the city that has shops, restaurants, and unique architecture. While you're in the French Quarter, visit the open-air restaurants near the river for some beignets, a fried pastry sprinkled with powdered sugar. New Orleans also has a large zoo, located in Audubon Park in the Uptown area. One of the main attractions in the city is the Garden District. You can ride the streetcars there to view beautiful old homes built during the 1800s.

The first sentence, "New Orleans has many tourist attractions," is the main point of the paragraph. All the remaining sentences support the main point by giving examples of tourist attractions found in New Orleans. Remember, however, that the main point may not always be stated in the first sentence of a paragraph.

Sometimes the gist is implied. In the following example, you have to "read between the lines" to figure out the main point. Paying careful attention to details can help you identify an implied main idea. Read the following paragraph and identify what it is mainly about.

A human bone is made up of hard tissue with tiny tunnels running through it. Blood vessels passing through these tunnels carry nutrients and oxygen to bone cells. The center of the bone is filled with marrow, a soft tissue. The marrow has several functions, including storing fat and making blood cells.

All the details in the paragraph above help you identify the implied main idea, which is "A human bone is a complex structure with many functions."

Here's an example of a "big picture" question similar to one that you might find on the TAKS ELA test. Return to "The Human Story Machine" on pages 20–22. Reread paragraphs 22 through 27. Then answer the question below.

"A Walk Along the Ocean" is mainly about —

A   how Hurley and Alice met

B   the wisdom of Alice's grandmother

C   a man who falls from the sky

D   a woman looking for true love

Choice D is the correct answer. This small story within the article is mainly about a woman looking for true love. Choices B and C refer to things mentioned in the story. Choice A is a detail from the article but is not in the story.

Identifying Supporting Details

As you have just read, the **details** in a selection support the primary message. In "A Walk Along the Ocean," the author writes that the man Alice had been dating broke up with her. This detail is **background information** that supports the main idea. If the man had not broken up with her, Alice might not have been searching for true love.

Some other ways that writers present details include

- **facts and figures** that answer questions such as *Who? What? When? Where? Which? Why?* and *How?* Newspaper stories and magazine articles often use facts and figures to explain a main idea.

- **sensory details** that tell how something *looks, sounds, feels, smells,* or *tastes*

Here's an example of a detail question that you might find on the TAKS ELA test. Return to "Long Walk to Forever" on pages 11–19. Review the story and then answer the question below.

What will happen to Newt as a result of going A.W.O.L.?

A   He will hitchhike back to Fort Bragg.

B   He will miss Catharine's wedding.

C   He will spend 30 days in the stockade.

D   He will serve seven more months in the army.

Choice C is the correct answer. Newt mentions this punishment in paragraph 99 of the story. Although we might assume that Newt will hitchhike back to Fort Bragg, it is not stated as a consequence of going A.W.O.L., making Choice A incorrect. Since Newt is not planning to attend Catharine's wedding anyway, Choice B is incorrect. Choice D is stated in the story, but not as a punishment for going A.W.O.L.

Objective 2

The student will demonstrate an understanding of the effects of literary elements and techniques in culturally diverse written texts.

The student expectations for Objective 2 tell what students should be able to do to move beyond a basic understanding of the text. This objective is aimed at answering the question "How does an author use literary elements and techniques to create meaning?" **Literary elements** are the essentials of a story: setting, characters, plot, and theme. You will find most of these literary elements in fiction and in some narrative nonfiction, such as autobiographies, biographies, and some essays. **Literary techniques** are devices such as foreshadowing, flashback, allusion, and symbolism that authors use to add texture and meaning to a story. These techniques shape the reader's understanding of the basic elements.

Literary elements include

- **setting**—the time and place in which the events of a story occur

- **characters**—the people or animals in a story (What are they like? Why do they do the things they do?)

- **plot**—the events of a story, including the conflict one or more characters face and how it is resolved

- **theme**—the central message of a story or the insight about life that a writer wishes to convey to readers

Literary techniques include

- **foreshadowing**—details that hint at the action to come in a story

- **flashback**—an interruption in the flow of a story to describe an event that took place at an earlier time

- **allusion**—a reference in a story to a literary or historical event, person, object, or idea with which the writer assumes the reader is familiar

- **symbolism**—the use of objects in a story to represent ideas or concepts, such as using a rose to stand for love

Analyzing Setting

The **setting** of a story is the place and time in which the events occur. Stories can be set in real or imaginary places. The events can happen in the *past*, *present*, or *future*.

©Photodisc

©Photodisc

Photo courtesy of the Library of Congress

Setting often plays an important role in what happens to the characters in a story and how they respond. It can influence a story's overall impact and meaning. As you read, notice whether the setting gives you clues to a character's background, beliefs, and motivation. For example, imagine a story in which a 16-year-old boy works each day in the dangerous coal mines of Kentucky. The setting may provide a motivation for him to move away and improve his life.

Here's an example of a setting question that you might find on the TAKS ELA test. Return to "Long Walk to Forever" on pages 11–19. Review paragraph 1. Then answer the question below.

> Since Catharine and Newt grew up next door to each other "on the fringe of a city," they probably —
>
> A never walked to school
>
> B rarely saw each other
>
> C had many friends in the neighborhood
>
> D depended on each other for companionship

The description of the setting in this question implies that the neighborhood is not as heavily populated as the city itself, and as a result the homes are more spread out. Choice D is correct because the reader can infer that there probably are not many young people in such a neighborhood. This also explains why Choice C is incorrect. Choice A is incorrect because there isn't enough information to draw this conclusion. Choice B is incorrect because, as next-door neighbors, they would have seen each other often.

Analyzing Characters

Readers usually meet the main character (or characters) in the first few paragraphs of a story. They learn about the character's traits, or characteristics, by paying attention to the character's words and actions, the character's appearance and mannerisms, and the way other characters react to him or her.

Here's an example of a question about character that you might find on the TAKS ELA test. Return again to "Long Walk to Forever" on pages 11–19. Review the text and answer the question below.

In paragraph 11, the author uses the description of Newt's appearance to —

A suggest that Newt wanted to get home in a hurry

B point out that Newt never cares how he looks

C prove how much Newt dislikes the army

D illustrate the fact that Newt likes to go for walks

Choice A is the correct answer. Newt left the army without permission and traveled a long distance to reach Catharine's house. His appearance shows that he did not take time to clean up before he knocked on Catharine's door. Choices B and C are incorrect because they are not supported by Newt's behavior in the rest of the story. Choice D is not why the author describes Newt's appearance.

Point of View

Every selection is written from a certain point of view. In **first-person point of view**, the story is narrated by one of its characters. As a result, the reader experiences only what that character knows and observes. In **third-person point of view**, the narrator does not participate in the action and is not a character in the story. If the third-person narrator focuses on only one character's thoughts and actions, the author is using a **limited point of view**. If the narrator knows about all the characters' thoughts and feelings, the story is being told from an **omniscient point of view**, the point of view used by the author in "Long Walk to Forever."

Describing and Analyzing Plot, Conflict, and Resolution

The **plot** is what happens in the story—the events that occur from beginning to end. The plot is usually built around a **conflict**, or problem, faced by one or more characters. The events in a story move toward the **resolution**, or solution, to the conflict or problem.

Let's look more closely at each of these elements.

Plot

The **plot** of a story tells what happens, when it happens, and to whom it happens. The sequence of events moves the plot forward. A story's plot usually includes the stages shown below.

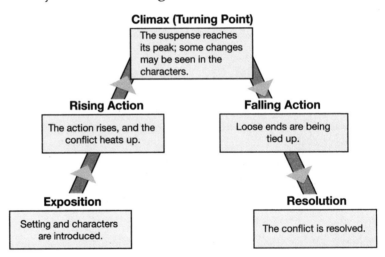

Climax (Turning Point)
The suspense reaches its peak; some changes may be seen in the characters.

Rising Action
The action rises, and the conflict heats up.

Falling Action
Loose ends are being tied up.

Exposition
Setting and characters are introduced.

Resolution
The conflict is resolved.

Here's an example of a question about plot that you might find on the TAKS ELA test. Return to "Long Walk to Forever" on pages 11–19. Review the story. Then answer the question below.

> The extra space inserted after paragraph 47 —
>
> A highlights a dramatic moment in the story
>
> B prepares the reader for a flashback
>
> C indicates the passage of several days
>
> D slows down the action of the story

Choice A is the correct answer. The extra space gives the reader a moment to reflect on an important event in the story—Newt has told Catharine that he loves her. Choice B is incorrect because the action continues forward in time after the extra space; a past event is not referred to. Choice C is incorrect because this story takes place during the course of one day. Choice D is incorrect because the action of the story picks up at this point.

Conflict

In most stories the main character faces a **conflict**. As you know, this struggle is often between two characters. Conflict can also occur

- within a single character (for example, a young woman longs to be independent but is afraid to act without her parents' advice)

- between a character and a force of nature (for example, an explorer battles a blizzard)

- between a character and society (for example, a young attorney battles to change a law)

Here's an example of a conflict question that you might find on the TAKS ELA test. Return to "Long Walk to Forever" on pages 11–19. Review the story and answer the question below.

Catharine makes sensible speeches to Newt in order to —

A hide her dislike of him

B pledge her love to him

C capture his attention

D control her feelings

Choice D is the correct answer. It reveals the story's conflict: Catharine loves Newt but is engaged to be married to someone else. By making "sensible speeches," she denies her feelings about Newt. Choice A is incorrect because Catharine loves Newt. Choice B is incorrect because Catharine does not pledge her love to Newt through her words. Choice C is incorrect because Catharine already has Newt's attention.

Resolution

A story usually ends when the conflicts faced by the main characters are resolved. In the **resolution** of a story, the loose ends are tied up, whether or not the characters "live happily ever after." In "Long Walk to Forever," the conflict is resolved when Catharine admits to herself that she loves Newt.

Recognizing Theme

The **theme** of a literary work is its underlying message. A theme is a central insight that the writing communicates about life or human nature. Sometimes a text will present more than one theme. "Long Walk to Forever," for example, addresses the themes of romantic love, the difficulty of relationships, and the consequences of acting spontaneously.

> A theme of the short story is "Don't take others for granted."

> The book's primary theme is "Working together is better than working alone."

> "The destructive power of jealousy" is one theme of the movie.

> I think a theme of the play is "Humor can improve a difficult situation."

Some themes are clearly stated in a selection. Others are not. In recognizing the theme of a story, careful readers look at how other story elements—setting, characters, and plot—work together to point to a theme. Sometimes the title of a story is a good clue to a theme.

One way to confirm a theme of a selection is to be able to justify it with supporting evidence from the text.

Here's an example of a theme-based question you might find on the TAKS ELA test. Return to "The Human Story Machine" on pages 20–22. Review the text and then answer the question below.

Which of the following sentences from "A Walk Along the Ocean" best expresses a theme of the story?

A *Well, this is all pretty rotten.*

B *But how will she ever find true love?*

C *Maybe he will fall from the sky, or maybe he will come from beneath the waves.*

D *For there are plenty of fish in the sea, and many men, too.*

Choice D is the correct answer. At the beginning of the story, Alice is confused and unhappy because a man has broken up with her. At the end of the story, the writer predicts that Alice will meet another man and fall in love with him. Choice D addresses this important idea. Neither Choice A, B, nor C is the best expression of theme for "A Walk Along the Ocean."

Using Text to Defend Responses

There are several ways to demonstrate your understanding of something you have read. You might retell the story or summarize it. You might make a statement and then quote from the text to support your statement.

... and Tonya knew she had made the right decision.

O.K., so your classmate says that the character in the story made the right decision. Are you going to take his word for it? What if you want some proof? As a classmate of this student, you might ask this question:

"What evidence do you have that Tonya made the right decision?"

The student then opens the book and reads from the last chapter:

Tonya felt fulfilled in her new role as a stepmother and a resident of a large city. She took a morning job at a bookstore and spent her afternoons taking the children to museums, libraries, and parks. She loved the quirky little apartment that she and Nathan had found, even though it seemed she was always busy cleaning up spilled juice, picking up puzzle pieces, and wiping noses when she was there. And, of course, she loved Nathan more than ever.

Below is an example of a text-support question that you might find on the TAKS ELA test. Return to "Long Walk to Forever" on pages 11–19. Review the story. Then answer the question below.

Which line from the story shows that Catharine knows her relationship with Newt is changing?

A *"I just mean this is all so unexpected."*

B *Somewhere far away an automobile starter nagged and failed, nagged and failed, fell still.*

C *"Do you have an idea how offensive you're being?"*

D *Catharine let Newt sleep for an hour, and while he slept she adored him with all her heart.*

Choice D is correct. Catharine finally acknowledges her true feelings for Newt while he is asleep, even though she doesn't express her feelings to him. Choices A and C are statements Catharine makes to Newt, but they do not express her newfound love for him. Choice B is symbolic of the change that is about to take place, but a careful reading shows that it does not symbolize Catharine's *awareness* of her feelings for Newt.

Understanding Literary Language

Has a song ever caused you to remember a past experience? If so, then you know that the different melodies and words of songs can have profound effects on people. A song can cause you to think of a favorite person, for example, or to relive a cherished memory. Authors hope to elicit similar responses in their readers with the words they choose. They select words with great care in order to evoke certain emotions and images and to demonstrate to their readers the rhythm, beauty, and flexibility of language.

Below is an example of a question about literary language that you might find on the TAKS ELA test. Return to "The Human Story Machine" on pages 20–22. Review paragraph 5 and answer the question below.

In paragraph 5, the author uses a simile to —

A show that he was eager for the group's approval

B prove that he can act as well as he can write

C indicate that he was trying to make the group laugh

D describe his fear of trying new things

In this paragraph, the simile compares Hurley to "a dog waiting to be petted." Answer Choice A is correct. Hurley is unsure of his idea and wants to try it out on his writers' group. Like a dog, he hopes to receive their approval. Choices B and C are incorrect because there is no evidence to support them in the paragraph. Choice D is incorrect because the simile does not describe Hurley's fear.

Connecting Literature to Historical Context

For some selections, it's important to know the **historical context**, or the key factors of life in the time period and place in which a literary work is set. The customs and attitudes reflected in a work may be very different from those of today. Knowing this information will help you understand key points about the selection's setting, background, and culture as well as the motivation of its characters.

Photos courtesy of the Library of Congress

For example, suppose you're reading a story about teenagers growing up in the segregated South in the 1940s. Knowing about the racial tension of the period and about the events that led up to World War II will help you better understand the story. In the same way, understanding important issues and common viewpoints from a certain period will help you analyze a piece of writing written during that period.

It's just as important to understand the context of some current pieces of writing. If you're reading an editorial in the newspaper about a local physical education requirement for schoolchildren, it may help your understanding to know about current nationwide trends in childhood obesity.

Many times if the context of a written work is important to understanding the work but is unclear, a brief explanation will introduce or be included in the selection. Writers for newspapers and newsmagazines often provide context for readers in the first few paragraphs of their articles.

Understanding Literary Terms

Authors have several ways to shape a reader's understanding of characters, events, and themes. These are a writer's "tools of the trade." Some of these are listed below.

Mood

The overall feeling or atmosphere that a writer creates for a reader is called **mood**. Specific words or phrases, such as "deepening gloom" or "sun-kissed radiance," can contribute to the mood of a work, as can figurative language, repetition, and other literary devices.

©John Lund/CORBIS

Foreshadowing

In **foreshadowing**, a writer hints about something that may happen in the future. Foreshadowing can arouse the reader's curiosity or build suspense.

Flashback

A **flashback** interrupts a story to relate an event that occurred in the past. Flashbacks often explain a character's present behavior by revealing an event from his or her past.

Irony

Irony involves a difference between what appears to be and what really is. In **verbal irony** a character says the opposite of what he or she means. In **irony of situation**, an event or situation turns out to be different from what the reader expects. In **dramatic irony** there's a difference between what a character says or thinks and what the reader knows is true. Through the use of irony, writers remind readers that life is unpredictable.

©CORBIS

46

Dialogue

Conversation between two or more characters is known as **dialogue**. Writers use dialogue to bring characters to life and to give the reader a sense of the characters' voices. The words spoken or thought by characters are usually set off with quotation marks.

Symbolism

A symbol stands for something beyond itself. Writers often use **symbolism** to indicate an important idea in a story. For example, seasons can symbolize the passing of time; a snake can symbolize evil.

Below is an example of a question about literary terms that you might find on the TAKS ELA test. Return to "Long Walk to Forever" on pages 11–19. Review paragraph 31 and answer the question below.

Why can Newt's response in paragraph 31 be described as ironic?

A He hopes to break Catharine's engagement.

B He wants to give Catharine a beautiful gift.

C He hasn't met Catharine's fiancé.

D He won't be able to attend Catharine's wedding.

Choice A is the correct answer. Although Newt says that he came to find out Catharine's silver pattern, he really came to ask her to marry him. Choice B may be tempting to some students because Newt talks about buying the couple a spoon. However, careful readers will look for the meaning beyond these words. Choices C and D are incorrect because they are not ironic.

Objective 3

The student will demonstrate the ability to analyze and critically evaluate culturally diverse written texts and visual representations.

The student expectations for Objective 3 tell what students should be able to do to move beyond the literal meaning of a text. Students should

- develop an understanding of a text that allows them to think critically about it

- connect what they already know to information in the text

- become independent thinkers by considering reasons that they may agree or disagree with a text

Objective 3 is aimed at two critical-thinking skills—analysis and evaluation.

To analyze a text, break it down and think about its fundamental elements, or parts. Then consider how these elements add to the text's overall meaning. For example, you may notice that an author has organized a magazine article by first discussing a problem and then explaining several solutions. Noticing this organization helps you identify the author's main points or arguments. You may also notice that the author uses words with connotations of urgency to describe the problem. These words help you determine the way the author feels about the subject.

To evaluate a text, you make judgments about the value of the text for a given purpose. For example, after reading a magazine article about a problem and solutions, you may decide that one solution is superior to the others. You may even decide to apply the solution in your own life.

Students must also be able to analyze and evaluate media messages, such as those from television, radio, magazines, newspapers, advertisements, billboards, posters, and websites. For example, you might ask questions such as

"What is the main point of the message?"

"What is its purpose?"

"How well does the message achieve its purpose?"

Analyzing Text Structures

As authors plan their writing, they select organizational patterns, or text structures, to arrange and link their ideas. Identifying the underlying organization of an entire text, as well as that of paragraphs or sections within the text, will help you better understand the meaning of the text. One common organizational pattern is **chronological order**, the organization used in many narratives. Authors using chronological order tell the events in the order in which they happen. Other text structures include compare and contrast, cause and effect, and problem and solution.

Authors use the **compare-and-contrast** pattern to compare two or more people, objects, or ideas. Suppose an author wants to compare the benefits of having a pet dog with the benefits of having a pet cat. He or she may begin by describing all the benefits of having pet dogs and follow this with a description of all the benefits of having pet cats. Or the author might select one benefit, such as companionship, and discuss how that applies to both animals before moving on to the next benefit.

With **cause and effect**, an author may describe a single cause and its effect or a series of causes and effects. Suppose an author is writing a narrative about a pet dog. Within the narrative she writes a paragraph using the pattern of cause and effect to describe an incident in which the dog disturbs a pile of papers on her desk. This, in turn, causes her to misplace one important page of a long report.

Fido certainly caused a mess!

Now suppose the same author is asked to write a short article about pets and fleas. She begins the article with a paragraph detailing the dangers of fleas—a problem. In the next paragraph she includes details describing types of flea collars and their effectiveness—a solution. She has structured her text with the **problem-and-solution** pattern.

Here's an example of a question about cause and effect that you might find on the TAKS ELA test. Return to "The Human Story Machine" on pages 20–22. Review paragraphs 22 through 27 and then answer the question below.

Why is "A Walk Along the Ocean" Dan Hurley's favorite story?

A It was the first instant novel he wrote.

B He wrote the story for the woman who later became his wife.

C The story combines fact and fiction.

D People applauded when he read the story about Alice.

Notice that the word *why* in the question signals a cause-and-effect relationship. When you look for the reason, or cause, that the story is the author's favorite, you see that Choice B is the correct answer. Choice A is not true because the author had written other instant novels before "A Walk Along the Ocean." Choices C and D are not reasons for the story becoming the author's favorite.

Making Inferences, Drawing Conclusions, and Making Predictions

You have probably noticed that authors do not always tell you everything directly. For example, instead of telling you that a character is bored, an author may write, "Elise stared blankly into space."

©Reg Charity/CORBIS

Making Inferences and Drawing Conclusions

To draw meaning from a text, you sometimes must piece together details in the text with information based on your own experiences. In other words, you must combine **explicit** ideas, those that are expressed directly, with **implicit** ideas, those that are not expressed directly but can be understood. When you figure out things by "reading between the lines," you are **making inferences**. When you make a series of inferences, you may draw a more general **conclusion**, or a deeper, more complete understanding of the text.

Making Predictions

"Reading between the lines" will also help you **make predictions**. When you make a prediction about what will happen next in a story, you stay actively involved in your reading. You can also make predictions about what will happen after a story ends. To make predictions, it's helpful to notice

- how characters react to problems
- important details about plot, setting, and character
- foreshadowing, or hints about what might happen later in the story

Here's an example of a question about making inferences and drawing conclusions that you might find on the TAKS ELA test. Return to "The Human Story Machine" on pages 20–22. Review paragraph 16 and then answer the question below.

Writing 60-second novels hasn't bored Hurley yet probably because —

A he enjoys pretending to be Superman

B he gets invited to many events

C people pay him well for the stories

D everyone's story is different

Choice D is the correct answer. This question asks you to make an inference. You must conclude that Hurley enjoys writing 60-second novels because he enjoys the variety that it brings. He enjoys talking to different people and learning about their lives. Choice A is incorrect because Hurley doesn't really pretend to be Superman. Choices B and C are incorrect because, although they may be true, they do not get at the heart of the reason that Hurley isn't yet bored.

Analyzing Across Texts

Sometimes you will need to use your analytic skills on more than one selection. When you see a play that has been adapted from a novel you enjoyed or you read two articles on the same topic, you cannot help making mental comparisons between the two works. The TAKS ELA test will ask you to perform this type of analysis as well. But remember, evidence to support your analysis must be present in **both** selections.

Here's an example of a cross-text item you might see on the TAKS ELA test. Review "Long Walk to Forever" on pages 11–19 and "The Human Story Machine" on pages 20–22, thinking about the main characters in each selection. Then answer the question below.

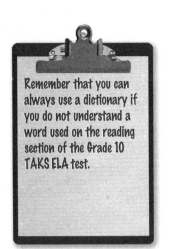

Remember that you can always use a dictionary if you do not understand a word used on the reading section of the Grade 10 TAKS ELA test.

> Which of the following traits do both Newt and Dan Hurley possess?
>
> A Shyness
>
> B Curiosity
>
> C Perseverance
>
> D Sarcasm

Choice C is the correct answer. In both selections, we see Newt and Dan Hurley overcome great odds to achieve their heart's desire. Choice A applies to Newt but not to Dan Hurley, while Choice B may be more appropriate for Hurley than for Newt. Hurley is portrayed as being very sincere, so Choice D is incorrect.

Identifying Author's Purpose

Authors have not only a variety of ways to organize what they write but also a variety of reasons for writing. Perhaps they want to inform the reader about an issue that is important to them, such as good nutrition. Or maybe they just want to share a humorous event. You can usually discover an **author's purpose for writing** by asking yourself, "Why did the author write this story? this editorial? this poem? this article?"

Some of the reasons that authors write include

- to entertain (for example, a story about a teacher who learns from his students)
- to inform or explain (for example, an article about economic changes in Asia)
- to express (for example, a journal entry about falling in love)
- to persuade (for example, an editorial in favor of creating bike lanes on a city street)

Authors also have a purpose for selecting specific words as they craft phrases, clauses, and sentences. For example, an author who is writing instructions (to inform) may choose words that emphasize order and precision, while an author who is writing a mystery (to entertain) may select words that emphasize suspense.

Sometimes an author has more than one purpose for writing. Think about "The Human Story Machine." Since it's an autobiographical nonfiction piece, you know that one of its purposes is to inform. However, because it's very engaging, you can conclude that it also has another purpose—to entertain.

Below is an example of a question about author's purpose that you might find on the TAKS ELA test. Return to "Long Walk to Forever" on pages 11–19. Review paragraphs 16 and 80 and then answer the question below.

> In paragraphs 16 and 80, the author uses the words *rosy* and *red* to describe Catharine's complexion in order to show the reader how easily —
>
> A   her face gets sunburned
>
> B   emotions appear on her face
>
> C   she becomes ashamed
>
> D   Newt can make her angry

Choice B is correct. In the middle of the story, Catharine feels awkward when she realizes that her love for Newt shows on her face. The author chose the words *red* and *rosy* to emphasize this character trait. Choices A and C are incorrect because the text doesn't indicate that Catharine gets sunburned or becomes ashamed. Choice D is incorrect; even though Catharine pretends to be angry at Newt, she really loves him.

Author's Craft

Authors make deliberate choices in the words they use, the way they structure a piece of writing, and the tone they create in a selection. These choices are elements of the **author's craft** and lead the reader to feel and react in ways that the author intends.

©Philip Gould/CORBIS

Eudora Welty

Here's an example of a question about author's craft similar to one you might see on the Grade 10 TAKS ELA test. Return to "Long Walk to Forever" on pages 11–19 and review paragraph 157. Then answer the question below.

The author uses four short sentences in paragraph 157 because —

A Newt is not willing to spend much energy pursuing Catharine

B he wants to emphasize the drama of the moment

C repetition is an important device in persuasive writing

D Catharine has always known that she is in love with Newt

Choice B is correct. The short sentences emphasize the importance of the moment. Choice A is not supported by the text. Newt has gone to a great deal of effort to talk to Catharine. Although repetition can be an important device in persuasive writing, "Long Walk to Forever" is not an example of persuasive writing, so Choice C is incorrect. Choice D is not supported by the text. Catharine does not know at first that she loves Newt.

Credibility of Information Sources

When you read an opinion piece in a newspaper, you know that you're reading one person's opinion. As a result, you may check the author's credentials at the bottom of the article to find out whether the person is a credible source. As you do this, you ask yourself, "Does the author's background make him or her an authority on this subject?"

When you check the **credibility** of information sources, you make a judgment—*Is this source believable?* To make this judgment, you might consider asking these questions:

- What are the author's motives for writing?
- What is the author's attitude toward the subject?
- What is the author's point of view on the subject?
- Does the author support opinions with sound and credible evidence?
- How current is the information he or she provides?

As you know, not all sources are reliable. One place where you might find *unreliable* sources is the Internet. When you visit a website for factual information, check its source before you begin reading. If it's "Pamela's Home Page," skip it. If it's *National Geographic*, read on. Sites with Web addresses that end in the following are often reliable sources:

- .edu (education)
- .gov (government)
- .mil (military)

Here's an example of a question about credibility that you might see on the TAKS ELA test. Review "The Human Story Machine" on pages 20–22 and then answer the question below.

The author's observations about writing "instant novels" are credible because —

A he conducted careful research before he began writing the article

B he is the first person to write instant novels

C the article is based on his own life

D he has read many instant novels

Choice C is correct. The article is autobiographical; therefore, its source is reliable—the author tells about experiences he knows about firsthand. Choice A is incorrect since we know that the author didn't need to conduct research about his own firsthand experience. Nothing in the article supports Choice B or Choice D.

Modes of Persuasion

Persuasive text is a type of writing in which the author tries to convince you to think or act in a certain way. In addition to advertisements and opinion pieces in newspapers, you'll find persuasive writing in speeches, books, and magazines—even movies.

Modes of persuasion are the various tools authors use to influence readers. Some of these modes, or forms, appeal to a reader's powers of logic. Others appeal to a reader's emotions.

Persuasive writing that appeals to a reader's powers of logic usually

- states an issue and the author's position

- gives opinions or claims that have supporting reasons or facts

- has a reasonable and respectful tone

- answers opposing views

Persuasive writing may use faulty reasoning. Such writing may include

- **overgeneralization**—This writing uses conclusions based on too little evidence. For example, "Two girls at school wore bell-bottoms yesterday. These bell-bottom pants are the style of the season. Everyone's wearing them."

- **circular reasoning**—This writing attempts to support an opinion by just repeating the opinion in different words. For example, "You should study hard because studying hard is something students should do."

- **faulty cause and effect**—Writing that contains faulty cause-and-effect reasoning suggests that Event A caused Event B just because Event B happened after Event A. For example, "When we planted a flower garden in our yard, more cats began to visit. The cats must like the flowers."

Persuasive writing that appeals to a reader's emotions may try to convince the reader of a position based on

- **individual experience**—For example, a writer may try to convince his or her audience that smoking is bad by describing how smoking has affected the writer in a negative way.

- **universal experience**—For example, a writer may make an emotional appeal based on something that everyone has experienced. "Cell-phone use while driving should be illegal! We've all seen drivers not paying attention to the traffic while they chatter away."

Persuasive writing that appeals to a reader's emotions can sometimes use faulty or deceptive techniques. These can include

- **loaded language**—Persuasive writing often uses words and phrases that have a strong positive or negative connotation. For example, "The recipes in the cookbook are simply heaven." Or in a speech a politician might describe his opponent's *plan* (positive connotation) as a *scheme* (negative connotation).

- **bandwagon appeal**—This type of writing urges readers to do or believe something because everyone else does. For example, "All Westside voters support Proposition 3—you should, too!"

- **testimonials**—Testimonials use famous people to endorse a product or idea. For example, "Actor George Nelson wears Racers every day."

Understanding modes of persuasion can help you evaluate information and make informed decisions.

Understanding Ideas and Relationships in Media

You have probably heard people blame the "media" for everything from too much violence in our cities to an increase in health problems. When people speak about **media**, they are referring to the variety of communication forms in our society today— television, radio, newspapers, magazines, and the Internet, for example. Except for radio, these forms all involve your visual sense, or sense of sight.

©Bettmann/CORBIS

When you read a short story, you take in ideas as words on a page. The ideas may be clearly stated, and the author may explain how the ideas relate to one another.

A television ad, on the other hand, may dazzle you with colorful images in fast motion, pounding music, and hypnotic words spoken by a professional announcer. After the ad is over, it's up to you to sort out the ideas and their meanings.

It's just as important to think about ideas presented visually—to evaluate the information you are viewing for purpose, content, and quality—as it is to evaluate what's on the printed page. To evaluate visual information, you can look for some of the same elements that you would look for in text, such as main idea, mood, theme, creator's purpose, and organization.

When you view visual media, remember that you may be taking in several ideas at once—and quickly. Take time to identify each idea. See if you can find relationships among the ideas. Use your own good judgment. Learn to be a critical viewer.

Here's an example of a question analyzing ideas in media that you might see on the TAKS ELA test. Review the Web page above and then answer the question below.

Which section of the website is most likely to contain advertisements?

A   Our Couple of the Week

B   What's Your Story?

C   People Search

D   Vacation Deals

Choice D is the correct answer. You can tell that this section of the website may contain advertisements because it uses the word "Deals," a loaded word. Choices A, B, and C seem to indicate sections of the site that offer additional information and stories. The words "most likely" in the question ask you to sift through the ideas and evaluate the **best** choice.

Understanding the Purpose of Media

The different forms of media are used to **entertain**, **inform**, and **persuade**. It's not always easy, though, to tell the purpose of a media message.

Suppose you're flipping through the pages of a magazine, and one page catches your eye. It appears to be an informative article with lots of text and few images. The title of the article is "New Exercise Program Breaks All Records." Charts and graphs show the benefits of using the exercise program, and there is a photograph of exercise equipment. You begin reading and notice that the tone of the article is serious. But as you read carefully, you come across phrases such as "disastrous effects" and "amazing benefits." Then you notice fine print at the bottom of the page that reads, "This is an advertisement." Those words are the key that the purpose of the article is to persuade.

Here are some questions to ask yourself about a visual representation (or image) to discover its purpose:

- How is the message presented?
- Is the presenter an authority?
- What kind of language does the representation use?
- Does the representation present a balanced picture?
- What are the underlying values of the representation?
- What is the source of the information? Is it up-to-date?

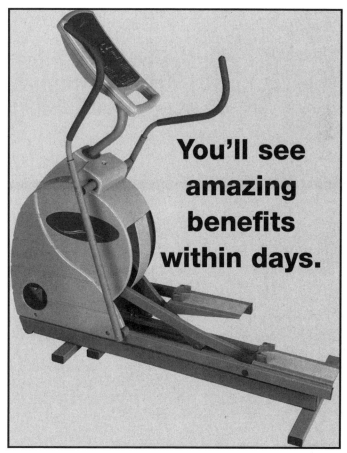

You'll see amazing benefits within days.

©CORBIS

The most important thing you should remember about analyzing a media image for its purpose is to trust your instincts. If you think the image is trying to sell you something, even an idea, it probably is.

Below is an example of a question about the purpose of media forms that you might see on the TAKS ELA test. Review the Web page on page 23. Then answer the question below.

What is the primary purpose of this website?

A   To persuade people to get married

B   To explain how to submit a story

C   To feature stories about how couples met

D   To provide vacation information

Choice C is the correct choice. You can tell that the site contains stories about how couples have met by looking at the photographs on the Web page and by reading the text. Choice A is incorrect because nothing on the Web page is about the benefits of marriage. Choices B and D are details that make up the Web page, but they do not state its purpose.

Finding the Main Point of a Media Message

You have learned to look for the gist or main idea in different types of text. You can also find the **main point of a media image**. However, finding a main point may sometimes be harder than finding out what a magazine article or encyclopedia entry is mostly about.

Photo courtesy of the Library of Congress

Media messages usually combine pictures *and* words. You can see these visual messages everywhere—on the Internet, on signs, even on cereal boxes. The images and words are selected carefully to pack a lot of ideas into a small space.

It is possible, though, to analyze media images—that is, to break them down into parts. Here are some tips for analyzing a media message to find its main idea:

- Study the visuals and text separately. Ask yourself what overall point each part of the image is making. Are the key points in each part the same?

- Look for the main idea behind the details.

- Try to summarize each part of the message. Do these summaries point to a main idea?

- Look for symbols in the image. Analyze what the symbols stand for.

Here's an example of a question about the main point of a media message that you might see on the TAKS ELA test. Review the Web page on page 23 and then answer the question below.

The stories on this website are primarily about —

A   second marriages

B   love at first sight

C   successful relationships

D   celebrity couples

Choice C is the correct choice. The words and images on the Web page tell you that it is about couples and love. The photographs show that the stories are about successful relationships. Choices A and D are incorrect because they are not found on the Web page. Choice B is incorrect because it relates to only a single story on the Web page.

Recognizing Persuasion in Media

Just as authors use certain tools in persuasive writing, media writers use tools to persuade viewers. Many media messages are designed to persuade but are disguised as entertainment or information.

Symbols

A **symbol** is an object that stands for something beyond itself. Symbols are often used in persuasive media messages because they appeal to the emotions. For example, clasped hands can symbolize cooperation, or an owl can symbolize wisdom. Be alert for symbols—particularly in advertisements—that try to tap into your hopes, dreams, or fears.

Loaded Terms

Media messages often contain words or statements that are chosen to draw an emotional response from the viewer. These **loaded terms** urge a viewer to respond in a certain way—for example, "Only the coolest teens wear Relics T-shirts."

I want to be cool. I'll buy a Relics T-shirt.

©CORBIS

Here's an example of a question about persuasion in media that you might see on the TAKS ELA test. Review the Web page on page 23. Then answer the question below.

Why do the creators of the website include pictures of hearts?

A To help viewers print information from the website

B To symbolize the website's content

C To connect viewers with vacation bargains

D To characterize the couple of the week

Choice B is correct. The website creators include pictures of hearts because hearts symbolize love and romance, the theme of the website. Choice A is incorrect because there is no place on the Web page directing users to print anything. Choices C and D are incorrect because, even though viewers click a heart to see vacation deals and to read about the couple of the week, the hearts appear in other places as well.

Short-Answer Items

In addition to the multiple-choice items for the Grade 10 TAKS ELA test, you will be asked to respond to several **short-answer questions**. Short-answer questions differ from multiple-choice questions in that they require you to write a short answer rather than simply select A, B, C, or D.

The short-answer questions on the Grade 10 ELA test

- address Objectives 2 and 3
- are based on the expository and literary selections
- may address one or both selections
- have many different possible answers

Short-answer responses may receive a score of 0 (insufficient), 1 (partially sufficient), 2 (sufficient), or 3 (exemplary).

When you take the Grade 10 ELA test, you will find that for each short-answer question, there are a number of lines on the answer document. If the question asks about one selection, five lines are provided. This number of lines means that your answers should not be very long—only a few sentences. If the question asks about both selections, eight lines are provided. These extra lines provide a little more space to compare selections.

How Do You Answer a Short-Answer Question?

You may be wondering how short-answer questions on a standardized test differ from the short-answer questions you have on classroom tests. Well, the answer is that they don't. To answer the short-answer questions on the Grade 10 ELA test, you should use the same strategies that you would use for any question that requires a short written answer. In other words your answer must be clearly written, **and** you must support your answer with evidence from the text. Examples of evidence include

- a direct quotation

- a paraphrase

- a specific synopsis or brief summary

Responding to short-answer questions on the ELA test may feel different from answering the same types of questions during an ordinary day at school. You may feel extra pressure during an exam. Here are some hints to help you relax and do your best on this part of the test. Many of these hints are useful for all parts of the TAKS ELA test.

- Take a deep breath and clear your mind. Then read the first question slowly and carefully. Make sure you understand what information the question is asking for.

- Think about how you could answer the question. Review the main points in your mind. You may want to make notes to use when writing your answer.

- Answer the question carefully and accurately. Do not write more information than the question calls for.

- Make sure that you support your answer with appropriate evidence from the selection or selections.

- Reread the question. Then review your answer. Make sure that your answer is complete and accurate.

Here are some examples of short-answer questions you might find on the Grade 10 ELA test. Return to "Long Walk to Forever" on pages 11–19. Review the story. Then read the question and sample responses below.

The analysis in the responses is in color. The text support is in black.

What is one conflict faced by Newt and Catharine in "Long Walk to Forever"? Support your answer with evidence from the selection.

Score Point 0

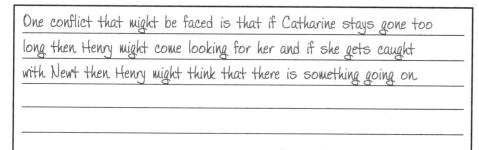

One conflict that might be faced is that if Catharine stays gone too long then Henry might come looking for her and if she gets caught with Newt then Henry might think that there is something going on.

There is no evidence in the story for this analysis, so it does not seem reasonable. In addition, no text support is offered.

Score Point 1

The analysis is clear, but no text support is offered.

> One conflict faced by Newt and Catharine was when Catharine realized her love for Newt. Since she was already engaged to be married to Henry, she had to figure out what she was going to do. Was she going to go ahead and marry Henry or call off the wedding and marry Newt?

Score Point 2

Reasonable analysis. Two quotations from the characters are offered as text support.

> One conflict faced by Newt and Catharine in "Long Walk to Forever" is that Newt loves Catharine but she is about to get married. Newt told her, "Remember how much I love you." She said, "What a crazy time to tell me you love me...my wedding is in one week."

Score Point 3

High-level analysis. The writer provides both quoted and paraphrased text support.

> One conflict facing Newt and Catharine is her confusion. Her marriage is only a week away when she discovers she loves Newt. She feels panicked by Newt's confessions of love and tries to deny they're true, but then she realizes "that a woman can't hide love." At the end she overcomes her confusion and runs back into Newt's arms when he calls her name.

Now review "The Human Story Machine" on pages 20–22 before reading the question and sample responses below.

> In "The Human Story Machine," has Hurley fulfilled his dream of becoming a novelist? Explain your answer and support it with evidence from the selection.

Score Point 0

I think he didn't, but he got another dream, and he liked that one better than his old dream.

The analysis is unclear and confusing. In addition, no text support is offered.

Score Point 1

Yes, I do believe that Hurley has fulfilled his dream of being a novelist due to the fact that he took an idea, started testing it, liked it, and has been writing his 60-second novels ever since.

Good start on analysis, but clear evidence from the text is needed for a higher score.

Score Point 2

In "The Human Story Machine," Hurley has fulfilled his dream of becoming a novelist and is very successful. He is so successful in what he does that "at this point, there aren't enough seats in Madison Square Garden to contain all the people he has written for." (paragraph 18)

Adds to analysis by commenting on Hurley's success. Text support is in the form of a direct quote with paragraph reference.

Score Point 3

Thoughtful analysis!
Can you see how the text
support really fits the
analysis?

Even if not in the traditional sense of "novelist," Hurley has fulfilled his dream. By sitting on the sidewalk and waiting for his stories to walk up to him, Hurley defines being a novelist in a new way. He writes, "the entire direction of my life veered off road. I had no idea what I had discovered... but I could see that it worked."

Now review both "Long Walk to Forever" and "The Human Story Machine" before reading the question and sample responses below.

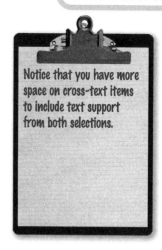

How does the idea of taking a risk apply to both "Long Walk to Forever" and "The Human Story Machine"? Support your answer with evidence from **both** selections.

Notice that you have more space on cross-text items to include text support from both selections.

Score Point 0

It's hard to take risks because then you're left with the consequences, but in the end, it's all worth it. In the story "Long Walk to Forever," he takes a risk and in the end it was worth it. The Human Story Machine also takes a risk and it is worth it.

The analysis is so general and repetitive that it could apply to almost any selection. No text support is present.

Score Point 1

In "Long Walk to Forever," the risk is that Catharine is dumping her husband-to-be for Newt without knowing if her life would have been better with Henry or if it would even last with Newt. In "The Human Story Machine," the risk is that he takes up with Alice, a stranger he doesn't even know, and ends up having a kid with her and living a happy life.

Nice start on analysis, but no text support is present.

69

Score Point 2

Analysis is present from both selections.
These quotes are short but to the point!

> In "Long Walk to Forever," Newt has run away from the army without telling anyone, just to meet Catharine. In paragraph 27, he says, "I'm what they call A.W.O.L." which is a military term for absent without leave. Hurley tries out his luck at making 60-second novels. If people don't like them or he isn't able to make them, people would forget him and his career would be over. For example in paragraph 9, people make fun of him and say, "what a gimmick."

Score Point 3

Nice analysis.
Text support includes both direct quotes and paraphrase.

> The idea of taking risks in both stories reveals to the reader that risk taking can be beneficial. Newt is "what they call A.W.O.L." and could face punishment in the stockades. He asks Catharine intrusive and at times offensive questions dealing with her marriage, and he even kisses her. His risk pays off at the end, though when "she ran to him, put her arms around him, could not speak." Hurley's idea of 60-second novels which another writer deemed "weird" eventually led to his marriage. This risk could have led to negative consequences, but it really paid off.

On Your Own

Now try these practice items. Then check your answers with the answer key and explanations beginning on page 78.

Use "Long Walk to Forever" on pages 11–19 to answer questions 1–8.

Question 1

In paragraph 83, the word *consternation* means—

A happiness and relief

B panic and fear

C concern and doubt

D surprise and dismay

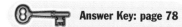 Answer Key: page 78

Question 2

Paragraphs 132 through 137 are mainly about—

A what happens while Newt is asleep

B how much Catharine loves Newt

C Catharine's decision to wake Newt

D where Catharine usually goes for a walk

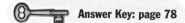 Answer Key: page 78

Question 3

Why has Newt returned to his hometown?

A To escape the army

B To see his mother

C To attend Catharine's wedding

D To talk with Catharine

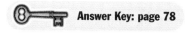 Answer Key: page 78

Question 4

Why does the author have Catharine open the door with a bride's magazine in her hand?

A To show how much she wants to be a bride

B To hint that she's getting married soon

C To indicate that she likes to daydream

D To explain why she's at home in the afternoon

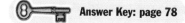 Answer Key: page 78

Question 5

In what way does Newt change most in the story?

A He overcomes his reservations about expressing his feelings for Catharine.

B He begins to realize that Catharine doesn't love him.

C He suddenly understands the consequences of going A.W.O.L.

D He admits that Henry Stewart Chasens is a better man than he is.

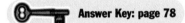 **Answer Key: page 78**

Question 6

Newt repeats the statement "One foot in front of the other—through leaves, over bridges" throughout the story. What does this quotation illustrate?

A Newt's determination

B Catharine's shyness

C Newt's love of nature

D Catharine's anger

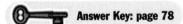 **Answer Key: page 78**

Question 7

In paragraph 155, Newt stares hard at Catharine probably because —

A she has admitted her love for him

B he looks directly at people when saying good-bye

C Catharine's face is so red that he is worried about her

D he wants to see whether she is telling the truth

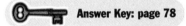 **Answer Key: page 78**

Question 8

What does the sound of the police siren in paragraph 35 represent?

A The risk that Newt has taken to see Catharine

B The sorrow Catharine feels for getting Newt into trouble

C The humor of Newt's predicament

D The confusion Catharine feels about marriage

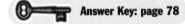 **Answer Key: page 78**

Use "The Human Story Machine" on pages 20–22 to answer questions 9–16.

Question 9

In paragraph 17, the word *confection* means —

A mixture

B length

C nonfiction

D interest

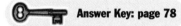
Answer Key: page 78

Question 10

Which element of paragraph 8 helps the reader understand the meaning of the word *circa*?

A *1983*

B *28-pound*

C *1953*

D *60-Second*

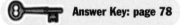
Answer Key: page 78

Question 11

The date April 24, 1983, is significant for the author because on that day he —

A met his future wife

B joined a writers' group

C became the 60-second novelist

D went to Madison Square Garden

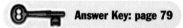
Answer Key: page 79

Question 12

Hurley can be described as someone who —

A takes risks

B doesn't care about others

C enjoys being alone

D doesn't listen well

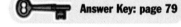
Answer Key: page 79

Question 13

In paragraph 13, Hurley uses the metaphor "the entire direction of my life veered off-road" to describe—

A his fear of reading his work in public

B the way he felt when he met Alice

C his mood as he begins writing each day

D the impact of writing his first 60-second novel

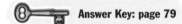 Answer Key: page 79

Question 14

How has being an instant novelist helped Hurley most in becoming a better writer?

A After 17 years his typing speed has increased.

B Noise no longer distracts him when he writes.

C He doesn't have to make up his own plots.

D He has been able to observe a great number of people.

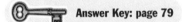 Answer Key: page 79

Question 15

One way the reader can tell that Hurley is serious about writing is that he—

A owns a 28-pound typewriter

B writes stories for his grandchildren

C belongs to a writers' group

D remembers every one of his stories

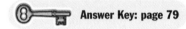 Answer Key: page 79

Question 16

In paragraph 13, Hurley refers to the crowd as "the ultimate deadline" because—

A everyone is waiting to hear the story

B no one will speak to him if he doesn't finish the story

C he continues to write stories so that everyone will applaud

D he doesn't like to be around people when he writes his instant novels

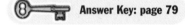 Answer Key: page 79

Use both "The Human Story Machine" and "Long Walk to Forever" (pp. 11–22) to answer questions 17 and 18.

Question 17

The couples in "Long Walk to Forever" and "The Human Story Machine" probably believe that—

A it's possible to fall in love at first sight

B they were meant to be together

C they would have been happier with other people

D relationships always proceed smoothly

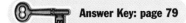 Answer Key: page 79

Question 18

Kurt Vonnegut, Jr., and Dan Hurley both—

A explain how much they want to write

B persuade readers to avoid risks

C point out the beauty of natural settings

D describe the unpredictability of romance

Answer Key: page 79

Use the Web page on page 23 to answer questions 19–21.

Question 19

The section called "We Meet Again" probably features couples who—

A met on blind dates

B were separated for a time

C lived a long time ago

D fell in love immediately

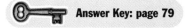 Answer Key: page 79

Question 20

Where would you find information about former couples of the week?

A Our Couple of the Week

B More Stories

C Couples Chat

D Story Archives

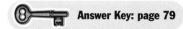 Answer Key: page 79

Question 21

The photo for "More Stories" indicates that the section includes stories about—

A weddings

B older couples

C active couples

D families

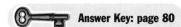 Answer Key: page 80

Question 22

How does Newt use language to cover his shyness? Support your answer with evidence from the selection.

_____

_____

_____

_____

_____

Answer Key: page 80

Question 23

What is one characteristic that makes Hurley a successful "human story machine"? Support your answer with evidence from the selection.

_____

_____

_____

_____

_____

Answer Key: page 80

Question 24

Look at the last line from "The Human Story Machine": "But then, no good story turns out the way you expect." How does this idea apply to both "Long Walk to Forever" and "The Human Story Machine"? Support your answer with evidence from **both** selections.

_____

_____

_____

_____

_____

_____

_____

_____

Answer Key: page 80

Reading Answer Key 🔑

"Long Walk to Forever"

Question 1 (page 71)

Choice D is correct. By using context, you can figure out that Catharine does not want Newt to know her true feelings. This context shows that *consternation* means "surprise and dismay." Choices A, B, and C are not correct because they do not represent Catharine's feelings.

Question 2 (page 71)

Choice A is correct. If you read this section, you see that it begins just as Newt falls asleep and ends when Catharine wakes him up. The paragraphs describe what happens during this time. Choices B and C are details in these paragraphs, but they do not describe what the section is *mainly* about. Choice D is not a detail from the story.

Question 3 (page 71)

Choice D is correct. This is why Newt has returned. Choices A, B, and C do not state the real reason that Newt returns to his hometown.

Question 4 (page 71)

Choice B is correct. The author uses this detail to characterize Catharine. She is holding a bride's magazine because she is getting married in a week. Choices A, C, and D are not supported by information in the story.

Question 5 (page 72)

Choice A is correct. Paying attention to details that show how a character changes in a story is a key to understanding the story's theme. When Newt is able to express his affection for Catharine, she recognizes that she would rather be with him than Henry. Choices B and D are not correct because they never happen in the story. Choice C is not correct because Newt knew the consequences of going A.W.O.L. all along.

Question 6 (page 72)

Choice A is correct. This question shows how dialogue can reveal character motivation. Newt is determined to approach Catharine and express his feelings for her, no matter the result. Choice B is incorrect because Catharine does not appear to be shy. Choice C is incorrect because the text never mentions that Newt loves nature. Choice D is incorrect because Catharine is angry at times, but Newt's statement does not illustrate this.

Question 7 (page 72)

Choice D is correct. This question asks you to analyze a cause-and-effect relationship. Newt stares at Catharine to "read" her expression. Choice A is incorrect because Catharine has not admitted that she loves Newt. Choice B is not supported in the text. Choice C is incorrect because nothing in the text suggests that Newt is worried about Catharine's face being red.

Question 8 (page 72)

Choice A is correct. This question asks you to make an inference. Newt makes a siren noise because he knows he will get into trouble when he returns to the army. Choice B is incorrect because Catharine isn't responsible for Newt's getting into trouble. Choice C is incorrect because nothing in the story suggests that Newt's predicament is humorous. Choice D is incorrect because Catharine does not become confused until later in the story.

"The Human Story Machine"

Question 9 (page 73)

Choice A is correct. The sentence says that Hurley's stories are a combination of "fact, fiction, fable and bibliotherapy." This context shows that *confection* means "mixture." Choices B and D are not correct because they do not make sense in the context of the sentence. Choice C is not correct because it is one part of the "mixture."

Question 10 (page 73)

Choice C is correct. The word *circa* is used in the story to indicate that the author's typewriter dates from about 1953. Choice A is not correct because it is a date unrelated to the typewriter. Choice B is not correct because it describes the weight of the typewriter. Choice D is not correct because it describes the word *novels*.

Question 11 (page 73)

Choice C is correct. It is the date on which the author became a 60-second novelist. Choice A is not correct because the author met his wife after this date. Choice B is incorrect because the author was already a member of a writers' group. The text does not indicate that the author went to Madison Square Garden, so Choice D is not correct.

Question 12 (page 73)

Choice A is correct. Hurley takes a risk by writing instant novels. He risks being ridiculed by people who do not like his stories or by people who think writing instant novels is a strange idea. Choices B, C, and D are not correct because nothing in the text supports these ideas.

Question 13 (page 74)

Choice D is correct. Writing his first 60-second novel changed the direction of Hurley's life by bringing him a career, wife, and family. Choice A is not correct because the text does not indicate that Hurley is afraid to read his work in public. Choice B is incorrect because the author does not meet Alice at this time. Choice C is incorrect because it does not accurately define what the metaphor describes.

Question 14 (page 74)

Choice D is correct. Writers observe people and use their observations to develop characters. Choices A and B are not correct because this information is not present in the text. Choice C is not correct because although Hurley gets ideas for his stories from the people he interviews, he still must make up his own characters.

Question 15 (page 74)

Choice C is correct. The question asks you to infer that people who belong to writers' groups want to improve their writing skills and are therefore "serious" about their writing. Choice A is not correct because it does not describe a way that an author would demonstrate being serious about writing. Choice B is not supported by information in the selection; Hurley does not yet have grandchildren. Choice D is incorrect because nothing in the text indicates that Hurley remembers all 25,000 of his stories.

Question 16 (page 74)

Choice A is correct. This question asks why the author chose certain words and phrases. Writers rarely have an audience as immediate as the crowds who wait to hear Hurley read a story seconds after he finishes it. Choice B is incorrect because this detail is not really part of the story. Choice C is not supported by information in the story. Choice D is incorrect because this information is not presented in the story. In fact, the reader can conclude that Hurley likes being around people as he writes.

"Long Walk to Forever" and "The Human Story Machine"

Question 17 (page 75)

Choice B is correct. The question asks you to make an inference based on evidence included in both selections. Choice A is not correct because the stories are not about love at first sight. Choice C is not correct because Hurley is happy with his wife, and readers can predict that Catharine and Newt will be happy. Choice D is not correct because neither selection is about relationships that proceed smoothly.

Question 18 (page 75)

Choice D is correct. The question asks you to think about the writers' reasons for writing. A theme of both selections is that romance can be unpredictable. Choice A is not correct because it applies only to Hurley. Choice B is not correct because neither selection is about avoiding risks. Choice C is not correct because neither selection is about nature.

"www.makeanewfriend.com"

Question 19 (page 75)

Choice B is correct. To answer this question, you must analyze the text and images on the Web page. Choices A, C, and D do not make as much sense.

Question 20 (page 75)

Choice D is correct. To answer this question, you must think about the text, especially the word *archives*. Choice A would not tell about former couples. Choices B and C would not tell about couples of the week.

Question 21 (page 75)

Choice D is correct. The image is a picture of a family. This tells you that this section is not limited to stories about couples. Choices A, B, and C are not correct because they do not relate to the photograph.

Short-Answer Items

Question 22 (page 76)

Sample Response: Newt uses irony and humor to avoid showing his feelings. When Catharine asks Newt why he left the Army without permission, he avoids telling her that he wants to marry her by responding, "I had to find out what your silver pattern is."

Question 23 (page 76)

Sample Response: Although Hurley is creative, energetic, and persistent, it is his ability to observe his customers that makes him most successful. As he says in paragraph 17, "But before I type the first word, I give them something else: my ears, my eyes, my total, 200-percent attention."

Question 24 (page 77)

Sample Response: The characters in both stories seem surprised by the way things turn out. Catharine professes her love for Henry and refuses Newt's proposal until the very end, when "She ran to him, put her arms around him, could not speak." Hurley had no idea how the "60-second novels" would change his life: "not only did my crazy idea to write stories on the street bring me a career, it brought me a wife and a family."

The student will, within a given context, produce an effective composition for a specific purpose that demonstrates a command of the conventions of spelling, capitalization, punctuation, grammar, usage, and sentence structure.

The student expectations for Objectives 4 and 5 tell what students should be able to do to communicate thoughts and ideas through written expression.

As you know, writing skills are important for a variety of reasons.

- They are critical for success in school.
- They help you clarify and focus your ideas.
- They are linked to strong reading skills.
- They give you an advantage in the workplace.

To demonstrate your writing skills on the Grade 10 ELA test, you will respond to a writing prompt by writing a composition in standard English prose.

What Are the Writing Prompts Like?

The writing prompts for the Grade 10 composition are linked by theme to the reading selections on the test. If you choose, you may refer to any or both of the selections in your response, but you are not required to do so. The prompts are designed to give you great flexibility. You will choose your own organizational strategy. For example, you may decide to write a series of causes and effects in response to the prompt, while a classmate may write an essay organized by problem and solution. The prompts also allow you to choose your own purpose for writing. You may want to persuade the reader to see your point, for example, while another student may choose to relate a personal experience. Read this sample prompt:

> Write an essay explaining how each person is responsible for finding his or her own "happy ending."

You can see that the above prompt is thematically linked to the selections "Long Walk to Forever" and "The Human Story Machine." This thematic link gives you two choices when you begin writing. You may refer to the selections in your composition, or you may choose not to refer to them. If you choose the first option, you can use examples and details from the selections as evidence to support your answer. Be sure to provide more than just a plot summary.

How Will My Composition Be Scored?

On the prompt page of the TAKS ELA test, a box like the one below will appear. The points listed in the box will help you remember what to think about as you write.

> REMEMBER — YOU SHOULD
>
> ❏ write about the assigned topic
>
> ❏ make your writing thoughtful and interesting
>
> ❏ make sure that each sentence you write contributes to your composition as a whole
>
> ❏ make sure that your ideas are clear and easy for the reader to follow
>
> ❏ write about your ideas in depth so that the reader is able to develop a good understanding of what you are saying
>
> ❏ proofread your writing to correct errors in spelling, capitalization, punctuation, grammar, and sentence structure

These points are the same ones that scorers will consider as they evaluate responses. As they read each response, scorers ask the following questions:

- Is the response about the assigned topic?
- Does the writing seem thoughtful and interesting?
- Do readers get a sense of who the writer is? Does the writing sound authentic and original?

- How well does each sentence contribute to the composition?

- Is the relationship between ideas clear? Do the introduction and conclusion add depth? Is there a sense of completeness?

- Are the ideas clear and easy to follow?

- Is the composition well organized? Is the progression of thought smooth and controlled? Are transitions used effectively?

- Are the ideas developed fully and thoughtfully?

- Has the response been proofread carefully?

- Do errors in spelling, capitalization, punctuation, grammar, usage, or sentence structure make the composition confusing or difficult to read?

Sample Compositions

The following sample compositions were written in response to the prompt below. They illustrate typical responses at score points 1, 2, 3, and 4, with 1 being the lowest and 4 being the highest.

> Write an essay explaining how each person is responsible for finding his or her own "happy ending."

REMEMBER — YOU SHOULD

❏ write about the assigned topic

❏ make your writing thoughtful and interesting

❏ make sure that each sentence you write contributes to your composition as a whole

❏ make sure that your ideas are clear and easy for the reader to follow

❏ write about your ideas in depth so that the reader is able to develop a good understanding of what you are saying

❏ proofread your writing to correct errors in spelling, capitalization, punctuation, grammar, and sentence structure

Score Point 1—Ineffective

Repeating the prompt over and over interferes with the writer's ability to make a connection with the reader.

Each person is responsible for finding his or her own "happy ending." Theres many ways how each person is responsible for finding their own happy ending. I am even responsible for finding my own happy ending.

One way a person is responsible for finding his or her own happy ending is no one else could find your own happy ending. All people have their own happy endings. A lot of people keep their happy endings to their selves. Each person is responsible for finding his or her own happy ending by achieving your goals in life. No other person can do it for you unless you put a lot of effort into it.

The introduction and conclusion do not add to the composition.

Transitions are included, but the ideas are still random and confusing.

Another way each person is responsible for finding his or her own happy ending is by achieving your goals in life. Once you have achieved your goals in life you then can be responsible for finding your own happy ending. Either to get married and have a family. What ever your happy ending is you have to have your life planned. Accomplishing your goals in life is basically what you have to do to find your own happy ending.

Some ideas are presented, but the writer simply repeats these ideas instead of telling more about them.

The last way each person is responsible for finding his or her own happy ending is how your life is going. If your life is going well you can be responsible for finding your own happy ending. If it is going bad you can still be responsible for finding your own happy ending. By staying out of trouble or making better achievements. Rich or poor everyone can be responsible for finding his or her happy ending.

Awkward sentences make the writing difficult to understand.

In conclusion many people consider an accomplishing their goals in life to be responsible for finding his or her own happy ending. Specific ways can find your own happy ending on responsibility. On the other hand good and better ways can find your own happy ending.

Score Point 2—Somewhat Effective

The composition as a whole does have some sense of completeness, but the progression of ideas is clearer in the third paragraph than in the second.

The writer uses examples from the literary selection to develop ideas.

> Everyone is responsible for finding their own "happy ending" to life. Attitude, personal decisions and choices, and inner determination are what people use to find their own true happiness in life.
>
> Attitude is a key factor in finding happiness in life. If a person holds a pessimistic outlook towards life he or she is not allowing him or herself to find any happiness in life. Happiness is different for everyone. One must decide what happiness is to themself before they may expect to attain it. Dreams are personal goals set to reach happiness. One must believe in themself and in their dreams to find happiness in life. Attitude is everything. To achieve happiness you must first believe.
>
> Life is an outcome of a series of decisions. Life is ultimately determined by the daily choices one makes, as is happiness. One must decide what happiness is to him or her and choose how to obtain it. In "Long Walk to Forever," by Kurt Vonnegut Jr., Newt decided he must tell Catharine how he feels. By doing so Newt is choosing to find his own happiness. Life's path is determined by the individual walking it. The determination of a person is very important to finding happiness. To succeed one must have great persistance and drive. In "Long Walk to Forever" Newt was successful in getting Catharine to show her feelings because he was so persistant; "One foot in front of the other — through leaves, over bridges." To find true happiness one must not be willing to give up.
>
> In conclusion, true happiness is found through attitude, decisions, and persistance. Therefore, each person is responsible for finding their own happy ending.

Repeating catch-phrases makes the writing sound stale and eliminates any sense of the writer's voice.

Some inaccurate words and phrases are present, but they do not cause the writing to be unclear.

Score Point 3—Generally Effective

For as long as I can remember, I have heard that everyone is responsible for his/her own happiness. As I have gotten older I have come to believe that this is true. I have also come to believe that a person's attitude has a great deal to do with their happiness.

Being in high school, you meet a lot of diverse people. You meet athletes, patrons of the arts, the so-called overachievers, and the general slackers. Some of these people are happier than others. For instance, many athletes and artists are happy because they are doing what they love and they are able to share the experience with others. However, many of the so-called overachievers are unhappy because they spend so much time trying to achieve their goals that they are not having any fun and they are stressed out. These are the choices that different people have made and every case is different, but they have chosen what they want to do and be and therefore are responsible for where those choices have led.

Also, I believe that if you truly want to be happy you will be. It is all a matter of attitude. If you think about being depressed all of the time than you will be. If you do nothing to try to change this way of thinking, then you are responsible for your lack of happiness. However, if you think you are happy then you will be or if you aren't but you try to be positive things can turn around. It's just like Peter Pan says, "Think happy thoughts." They can get you through anything.

As you can see every person is responsible for their own happiness. Their actions, attitudes, and willfulness are ultimately the deciding factors in their happiness. Everyone can be happy. It is just a matter of trying.

Describing the diverse groups of people in high school engages the reader.

Most of the writing contributes to the composition as a whole. The writer's thoughts progress steadily from sentence to sentence. Specific examples show the reader what the writer is saying.

The introduction and conclusion add some depth.

Writing mechanics are generally appropriate; the writer remembered to proofread!

Score Point 4—Highly Effective

The writer immediately engages the reader and maintains the connection throughout.

Each sentence clearly contributes to the composition as a whole. The writer uses the metaphor of a story to organize the composition.

The writer takes risks to develop interesting ideas.

The writer's choice of words, phrases, and sentence structures enhances the communication of ideas and lets the reader really hear the writer's voice.

Do you know what it means to "live happily ever after?" Most people don't. It means, "live happily from then on." It surprises me how many people do it without understanding that it is in fact what they are doing, living happily ever after, that is. How does one do that, find a happy ending?

To begin with, your story is exactly that: yours. The beginning is none of your fault, but as the tale goes on and on, it becomes more and more your responsibility to decide largely what happens next, mostly because you can. You are capable of a wondrous thing, of making choices to determine what happens next. There's only one problem about choices: it's the same thing that makes them wonderful. Lean closer to the paper and I'll whisper that dreaded word to you. Closer, please. Much better. Consequences.

Every option, action, thought, and choice has them. They may be good, they may be bad. The only thing they never are is avoidable. All those consequences pile up and wiggle around, affecting your life and changing the story and its ending. Your own choices determine whether your ending will be happy, not-so-happy, or put-it-away,-Daddy,-I-don't-want-to-hear-it-anymore. How'd you like to hear someone say that about your story? You know, the one you write every minute of every day. To really write your life story, there's something else you have to do: you alone are responsible for making your own choices. For some people, making choices is like breathing: habitual and somewhat necessary. For others, its like dancing: measured steps to complete it. For still others, making choices is like taking out the garbage: "Do I have to?" Either way, choices are yours: no one can make them for you any more than they can breathe for you. So make good choices with a tiny element of risk. It's like a small dash of Tabasco sauce; it gives your life flavor. Write a good story. I look forward to reading your happy ending.

The Writing Process

Even the best writers don't expect to produce a finished composition on their first attempt. They understand that writing is a **process** that involves several important steps.

© Jose Luis Pelaez, Inc./CORBIS

Jin has written a response to the prompt about happy endings found on page 84. Let's see how she took her composition through the following stages of the writing process:

✔ Prewriting

✔ Composing

✔ Revising

✔ Editing

✔ Publishing

Prewriting

Before Jin began her writing journey, she thought it would be helpful to have a road map to help guide her ideas. She used the graphic organizer below to organize her thoughts before she began composing.

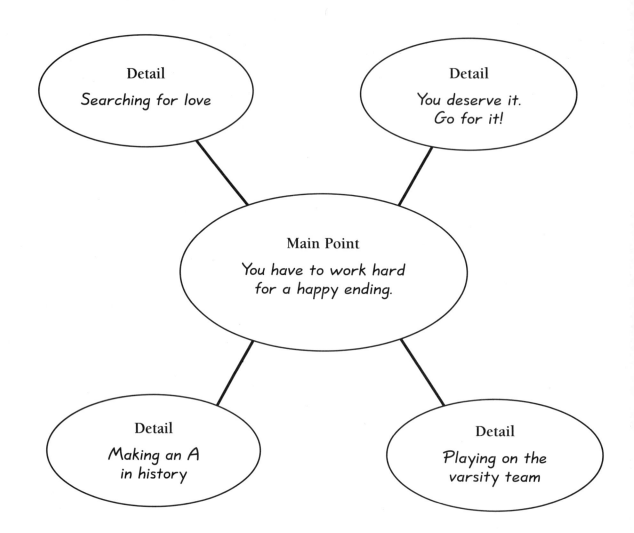

Detail

Searching for love

Detail

*You deserve it.
Go for it!*

Main Point

*You have to work hard
for a happy ending.*

Detail

*Making an A
in history*

Detail

*Playing on the
varsity team*

Composing

Using her prewriting chart, Jin wrote the following rough draft. She simply tried to get her thoughts down on paper "roughly" in the order she wanted them. (In this step Jin could take initial risks and be creative in the way she presented her ideas.)

> Love is only a four letter word but it holds so much power. Many people say love is ellusive and some say its where you least expect it but in the end aren't you responsible for finding or not finding it? For me when I think of a happy ending I think of love. After all, aren't some of the greatest fairytales like Snow White ended with love.
>
> In this world we only have one life and many people want to end it with a happy ending. So, you would think with all these people looking for a happy ending we would have more. However, you also have to factor in the fact that most people just sit around waiting for their happy ending to find them. Hello, wake up! A happy ending is like anything else you want in life. For example, say you want an A in history you don't just sit in the back waiting for you're A. You partisipate and study hard. Or say you want to make the varsity team. You don't stand against the wall and hope your coach see how good you are you go after it.
>
> In the end you control your life, and you only get one. Make it good.

Revising

When Jin's rough draft was complete, she began revising. In this step she concentrated on her ideas. Were they interesting, clear, and fully developed for the reader? She did not worry about correcting spelling, punctuation, capitalization, or grammar errors. That would come later.

Delete the entire introduction because it does not have any connection to what the essay is about: "hard work"!

Make this paragraph the introduction. It gives a clear explanation of the main idea of the response.

Delete "for example" because "say" clearly expresses the same idea. It makes the idea clearer.

Details add specificity. Fuller explanation of ideas adds depth.

More specific information adds depth to the response and makes it more interesting to the reader.

~~Love is only a four letter word but it holds so much power. Many people say love is ellusive and some say its where you least expect it but in the end aren't you responsible for finding or not finding it? For me when I think of a happy ending I think of love. After all, aren't some of the greatest fairytales like Snow White ended with love.~~

In this world we only have one life and many people want to ^have^ ~~end it~~ with a happy ending. So, you would think with all these people looking for a happy ending we would have more ^of them^. However, you also have to factor in the fact that most people just sit around waiting for their happy ending to find them. Hello, wake up! A happy ending is like anything else you want in life. ^You have to work for it.^ ~~For example,~~ say you want an A in history you don't just sit in the back waiting for you're A. You ^you^ partisipate ^in class^ and study hard ^for tests^. ~~Or say~~ ^If^ you want to make the varsity ^basketball^ team. You ^you^ don't stand against the wall and hope your coach see how good you are ~~you go after it.~~

In the end you control your life, and you only get one. Make it good. So when you make your A or score the winning basket you know you deserve that happy ending because you've worked hard for it—you made it happen.

You turn in your homework complete and on time. You take responsibility for your work. The classroom isn't the only place hard work pays off.

You practice your lay-ups, your dribbling, and your free-throws. Then you go to try-outs. Yes, it may be scary but you've worked hard and you know you're ready.

Simplify this awkward phrase.

Combining sentences adds variety to sentence structure.

Transition to link ideas and add depth to the conclusion.

Added information helps transition to the next idea.

Editing

After Jin's revision, she began the process of editing to locate and correct the errors in her writing that might interfere with her message. She used her dictionary often to help correct spelling errors.

Comma needed between independent clauses in a compound sentence.

Comma needed after a long introductory prepositional phrase.

Dash added to emphasize writer's voice.

Wrong word used. Incorrect homonym.

Change to make subject and verb agree.

Capitalize "say" because it is the first word of the sentence.

Correct spelling error.

Start a new paragraph for the new idea.

Comma needed between clauses in a compound sentence.

Comma needed after introductory adverb clause.

In this world we only have one life, and many people want to have a happy ending. So, you would think with all these people looking for a happy ending, we would have more of them. However, you also have to factor in the fact that most people just sit around waiting for their happy ending to find them. Hello—wake up! A happy ending is like anything else you want in life—you have to work for it. Say you want an A in history you don't just sit in the back waiting for your A, you participate in class and study hard for tests. You turn in your homework complete and on time. You ask for help if you need it. You take responsibility for your work. The classroom isn't the only place hard work pays off. If you want to make the varsity basketball team, you don't stand against the wall and hope your coach sees how good you are. You practice your lay-ups, your dribbling, and your free-throws. Then you go to try-outs. Yes, it may be scary, but you've worked hard and you know you're ready.

So when you make your A or score the winning basket, you know you deserve that happy ending because you've worked hard for it you made it happen. In the end you control your life, and you only get one. Make it good.

Compare this version to the rough draft on page 91.

Publishing

After Jin revised and edited her work, her composition was ready for the publishing phase. She copied her corrected version onto a clean sheet of paper, rereading it one final time.

> In this world we only have one life, and many people want to have a happy ending. So, you would think with all these people looking for a happy ending, we would have more of them. However, you also have to consider the fact that most people just sit around waiting for their happy ending to find them. Hello—wake up! A happy ending is like anything else you want in life—you have to work for it.
>
> Say you want an A in history. You don't just sit in the back waiting for your A, you participate in class and study hard for tests. You turn in your homework complete and on time. You ask for help if you need it. You take responsibility for your work.
>
> The classroom isn't the only place hard work pays off. If you want to make the varsity basketball team, you don't stand against the wall and hope your coach sees how good you are. You practice your lay-ups, your dribbling, and your free-throws. Then you go to try-outs. Yes, it may be scary, but you've worked hard and you know you're ready.
>
> So when you make your A or score the winning basket, you know you deserve that happy ending because you've worked hard for it—you made it happen In the end you control your life, and you only get one. Make it good.

On Your Own

Now you can try writing a composition using the prompt on the next page. Use the same writing process that Jin used when she wrote her composition. The following tips will help you remember the steps of the writing process.

✓ Prewrite

After you read the prompt, create a graphic organizer such as a word web, a cluster diagram, a chart, or an outline. You will find that putting your thoughts into a visual format will help you organize your ideas.

✓ Compose

After you have brainstormed ideas in the prewriting stage, you are ready to begin writing. Your first draft will probably be very rough. You should not expect your first efforts at writing to be perfect—in fact, the writing at this stage will be quite unpolished. Your main goal should be to get your ideas down on paper. Here are some guidelines for writing a rough draft:

- Decide on your purpose and audience before you begin.

- Allow plenty of space for later revisions. If you are using lined paper, you may want to write on every other line.

- Don't worry if your paper is messy or if it contains mistakes.

✓ Revise

When most of your ideas are down on paper, your draft is complete. After you have taken a breath, reread your draft all the way through one time. You may want to add or delete words, sentences, or even paragraphs. You may want to make certain words more specific. Write your changes between the lines or in the margins. Don't be shy about making big changes, such as rewriting the conclusion or moving a paragraph. As you revise, ask yourself these questions:

- Is my writing thoughtful and interesting?

- Am I sharing my ideas in my own way?

- Does each sentence contribute to my composition?

- Are my ideas clearly stated and easy to follow?

- Are my ideas developed in depth?

✓ Edit

Before you begin rewriting your composition, take a few minutes to proofread it. When you proofread, you add the final polish to your writing. Read through your paper and correct errors in spelling, capitalization, punctuation, grammar, usage, and sentence structure. Remember to use a dictionary.

✓ Publish

When you are convinced that your composition is complete and correct, copy it over as neatly as possible. When you have finished writing, reread your composition to make sure that you haven't left anything out or made mistakes in copying.

Sample Writing Prompt

Here's a prompt for you to write about on your own.

> Write a composition explaining what can happen when a person acts impulsively.

The information in the box below will help you remember what you should think about when you write your composition.

REMEMBER — YOU SHOULD

❑ write about the assigned topic

❑ make your writing thoughtful and interesting

❑ make sure that each sentence you write contributes to your composition as a whole

❑ make sure that your ideas are clear and easy for the reader to follow

❑ write about your ideas in depth so that the reader is able to develop a good understanding of what you are saying

❑ proofread your writing to correct errors in spelling, capitalization, punctuation, grammar, and sentence structure

---

Prewriting

Draft

Draft

Revised Copy

Revised Copy

The student will demonstrate the ability to proofread to improve the clarity and effectiveness of a piece of writing.

The clarity and effectiveness of a piece of writing are directly influenced by the writer's organization of ideas, sentence structure, standard English usage, and mechanics. To write effectively, you must understand how these components work individually and together.

> **Important Note**
>
> The revising and editing section of the TAKS test will assess your ability to improve a piece of writing that could have been written by one of your classmates. You will analyze the writing in terms of its
>
> - organization
> - sentence structure
> - standard English usage
> - mechanics
>
> This guide will offer instruction and review in each of these areas.

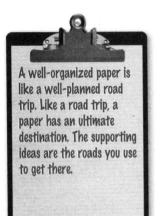

A well-organized paper is like a well-planned road trip. Like a road trip, a paper has an ultimate destination. The supporting ideas are the roads you use to get there.

Organization

To communicate effectively, a writer must organize and develop ideas in a coherent way. This means that main points should be well supported, ideas should be presented in a logical sequence, transitions should connect ideas, and no extraneous sentences should be included.

Supporting Sentences

Imagine that you have been learning about the availability of water on Earth. You have learned some interesting facts, including this one:

Drinkable water is hard to find.

Now you want to write about this idea. What kind of sentences do you need? You need **supporting sentences** to tell more about this idea.

Look at the sentences below. Mark the sentences that can be used to support the idea that drinkable water is hard to find.

_____ 1. Although 70 percent of Earth's surface is covered with water, much of that water is not fit to drink.

_____ 2. Other planets in the solar system are made up mostly of rocks and gas.

_____ 3. Ocean water is full of salt and other substances that make it almost impossible to drink.

_____ 4. The tallest mountain on Earth is Mount Everest in the Himalayas.

_____ 5. Underground aquifers make up less than 1 percent of Earth's water, while lakes and rivers make up even less than that.

_____ 6. The water we drink comes from lakes, rivers, and underground sources.

_____ 7. When water is heated to a certain temperature, it turns into a gas.

_____ 8. The next time you drink a glass of water, savor it for the treasure it is.

Which sentences did you mark? If you marked sentences 1, 3, 5, 6, and 8, you have plenty of support to write a paragraph about drinkable water on Earth. Sentences 2, 4, and 7 do not support the idea that drinkable water is hard to find. Readers don't need to know about the composition of other planets or when water turns into a gas. They don't need to know about the tallest mountain on Earth, either. These sentences present **extraneous** ideas. Extraneous ideas will confuse and distract your readers. They should not be included in your papers.

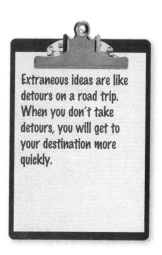

Extraneous ideas are like detours on a road trip. When you don't take detours, you will get to your destination more quickly.

If your writing does not follow a logical sequence, it is like taking a trip without a map. You may take a road that goes south when you need to go east. Eventually you will get to your destination, but it will probably take longer and you may get lost along the way.

Sequence/Progression

You've identified some sentences that can be used to support the idea on page 102 and some sentences that are not directly related to it. How do you organize the ideas you have selected into a logical, coherent paragraph?

First you must put the supporting sentences in an order that your readers will be able to follow and understand.

Let's start by writing the sentences you selected in the order they appeared on page 103.

> (1) Drinkable water may be harder to find than you think. (2) Although 70 percent of Earth's surface is covered with water, much of that water is not fit to drink. (3) Ocean water is full of salt and other substances that make it almost impossible to drink. (4) Underground aquifers make up less than 1 percent of Earth's water, while lakes and rivers make up even less than that. (5) The water we drink comes from lakes, rivers, and underground sources. (6) The next time you drink a glass of water, savor it for the treasure it is.

Read the paragraph aloud. Does it sound right? Are the sentences in a logical order? Since one of the sentences is out of place, the ideas do not flow logically. Which sentence is out of place in the paragraph above? Write the sentence on the lines below.

_____

_____

Sentence 4 talks about the percentage of Earth's water that can be found in aquifers, lakes, and rivers. We don't learn until sentence 5 that this is important because our drinking water comes from these places. This paragraph would make more sense if sentences 4 and 5 were switched.

Look at the paragraph now.

> (1) Drinkable water may be harder to find than you think.
> (2) Although 70 percent of Earth's surface is covered with water,
> much of that water is not fit to drink. (3) Ocean water is full of salt
> and other substances that make it almost impossible to drink.
> **(4) The water we drink comes from lakes, rivers, and
> underground sources. (5) Underground aquifers make up less
> than 1 percent of Earth's water, while lakes and rivers make up
> even less than that.** (6) The next time you drink a glass of water,
> savor it for the treasure it is.

By switching the placement of these two sentences, you have improved
the logical progression of thought in the paragraph. The paragraph
sounds better now, but it still seems to need work. Have you ever
finished writing and suddenly remembered a detail you forgot to
include? Take a look at this sentence:

> The four oceans—the Pacific, Atlantic, Indian, and Arctic—make
> up about 97 percent of the water on Earth.

If you wanted to add this idea to the paragraph, where would it most
logically fit? Remember that it has to fit in with the progression of the
other ideas in the paragraph.

This sentence talks about how much water is in the oceans, so it
should be near another sentence about oceans. Sentence 3 is about
oceans. Would this new idea make more sense before or after
sentence 3? It should precede sentence 3. Look at the paragraph with
this sentence inserted before sentence 3.

> (1) Drinkable water may be harder to find than you think.
> (2) Although 70 percent of Earth's surface is covered with water,
> much of that water is not fit to drink. **The four oceans—the
> Pacific, Atlantic, Indian, and Arctic—make up about 97 percent
> of the water on Earth.** (3) Ocean water is full of salt and other
> substances that make it almost impossible to drink. (4) The water
> we drink comes from lakes, rivers, and underground sources.
> (5) Underground aquifers make up less than 1 percent of Earth's
> water, while lakes and rivers make up even less than that. (6) The
> next time you drink a glass of water, savor it for the treasure it is.

The sentences now move in a logical progression, but they still do not
flow smoothly. That's because there are no transitions to connect the
ideas in this paragraph.

Transitions

Transitions alert your reader to what's coming next and connect ideas together in a way that makes sense. Transitions may be words, phrases, or complete sentences. Some common transition words or phrases are listed below.

For example,	In addition,
However,	In fact,
Unfortunately,	In other words,

Look at the paragraph on the previous page. Where could you add transition words or phrases to make the paragraph flow more smoothly? Here are some suggestions:

> (1) Drinkable water may be harder to find than you think. (2) Although 70 percent of Earth's surface is covered with water, much of that water is not fit to drink. (3) The four oceans—the Pacific, Atlantic, Indian, and Arctic—make up about 97 percent of the water on Earth. (4) **Unfortunately**, ocean water is full of salt and other substances that make it almost impossible to drink. (5) The water we drink comes from lakes, rivers, and underground sources. (6) **However**, underground aquifers make up less than 1 percent of Earth's water, while lakes and rivers make up even less than that. (7) The next time you drink a glass of water, savor it for the treasure it is.

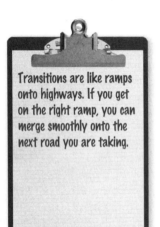

Transitions are like ramps onto highways. If you get on the right ramp, you can merge smoothly onto the next road you are taking.

> ### Important Note
>
> When you finish a piece of writing, ask yourself these questions:
>
> - Have I given plenty of support for my ideas?
> - Have I presented my ideas in a logical sequence?
> - Have I used transitions to connect my ideas?
>
> If you can answer yes to all these questions, you have probably generated a well-organized piece of writing.

Sentence Structure

Complete Sentences

The following are examples of complete sentences. The subject of each sentence is underlined once, while the verb is underlined twice.

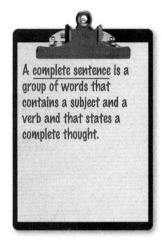

A complete sentence is a group of words that contains a subject and a verb and that states a complete thought.

- Two boys and a dog dash quickly through the woods in the moonlight.
- Covered from head to toe with mud, Alfred needed a good bath.

In the first sentence the subject comes at the beginning of the sentence, but that is not always the case. Notice that the subject in the second sentence comes in the middle.

Sentence Fragments

A **fragment** is a group of words that doesn't express a complete thought. Usually a fragment is missing either a subject or a verb, but a fragment can still be incomplete even if it has both a subject and a verb. Look at these sentence fragments:

- A strange box in a deep hole in the middle of the park.
- Was excited to find family mementos from more than a century ago.
- To a local museum, where they will be displayed for the public.

Since sentence fragments state incomplete thoughts, each of the fragments above must be missing something. What is each fragment missing? How can the fragments be corrected?

A strange box **was discovered** in a deep hole in the middle of the park.

In the first fragment the verb was missing. By adding the verb *was discovered*, we make this fragment a complete sentence.

> **The investigator** was excited to find family mementos from more than a century ago.

In the second fragment the subject was missing. By adding the subject *the investigator*, we make this fragment a complete sentence.

> **The mementos were donated** to a local museum, where they will be displayed for the public.

The third fragment didn't have a subject or a verb in the main clause. By adding the subject *the mementos* and the verb *were donated*, we make this fragment a complete sentence.

> ## Important Note
> People do not always speak in complete sentences. They can use their hands, vocal inflections, and facial expressions to communicate meaning. When you write, however, you have only the words on the page with which to communicate. That's why you must use complete sentences. You need to be sure your readers will understand what you are trying to say.

Run-on Sentences

Whereas a sentence fragment is missing something, a run-on sentence has too much of something. A run-on sentence has too many subjects and predicates. A **run-on sentence** consists of two or more complete ideas put together without the correct punctuation or capitalization. Run-on sentences are confusing because readers cannot tell where one thought ends and another one begins.

Look at this run-on sentence:

> Jake went to the mall to buy a new video game it was called *Mysteries of the Deep.*

The run-on sentence above is really two complete ideas. One idea is about Jake; the other is about the video game. Here's one way to correct the run-on:

> Jake went to the mall to buy a new video game. It was called *Mysteries of the Deep.*

It's often more effective to combine the ideas in a run-on sentence. Here's a way to combine the ideas in the run-on sentence about Jake:

> Jake went to the mall to buy a new video game called *Mysteries of the Deep*.

When the ideas in a run-on are closely connected, you can also use a semicolon to correct the run-on.

> Jake went to the mall to buy a new video game; it was called *Mysteries of the Deep*.

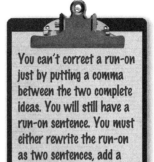

You can't correct a run-on just by putting a comma between the two complete ideas. You will still have a run-on sentence. You must either rewrite the run-on as two sentences, add a semicolon, or combine the ideas to form one sentence.

Try It

Look at the following sentences. Can you find some run-on sentences? Mark each run-on.

_____ 1. We went to the park to watch the play the performance was to begin at dark.

_____ 2. The sun went down, the curtain opened, and the audience cheered.

_____ 3. Max stared blankly at the crowd he had forgotten his lines.

_____ 4. The director gave him a cue, and the rest of the production was magnificent.

_____ 5. I think I'll try out for a part next year being onstage looked like fun.

Did you identify sentences 1, 3, and 5 as run-on sentences? How can you correct these run-ons? Remember that you can always rewrite a run-on as two separate sentences, but sometimes it's more effective to use a semicolon or find a way to combine the ideas.

_____

_____

_____

_____

_____

_____

Answer Key: page 149

Awkward Sentences

Some sentences are complete but still confusing to readers because the ideas are not expressed clearly. This kind of sentence is called an **awkward** sentence.

> Ryan had to transport the equipment, so his mother let him take it to the baseball field in her truck, which she let him borrow.

Because of the way the sentence in the box is written, the reader has to work harder than necessary to figure out exactly what the writer means.

- Did Ryan transport the equipment before he went to the field?
- Who is borrowing a truck?
- Whose truck is being borrowed?

Think about the ideas in the sentence above. How can you rewrite the sentence so that its meaning is clear and it's easier to read? Here is one way:

> Ryan's mother let him borrow her truck so that he could transport the equipment to the baseball field.

Misplaced Modifiers

A **modifier** is a word or phrase that adds detail to the meaning of another word or phrase. Some sentences are confusing because a modifier is in the wrong place.

> I read about some Arctic explorers who got lost in a library book.

Did the explorers really get lost in a library book? Of course not, but that's what the sentence says. The phrase *in a library book* is supposed to tell more about where *I read*, not about where *some Arctic explorers got lost*.

Look at the corrected sentence below.

> I read in a library book about some Arctic explorers who got lost.

Now the modifier is in the right place.

Try It

The sentence below has a misplaced modifier. Rewrite the sentence so that its meaning is clear.

Lina and her sister heard the howl of the wolf shivering under their covers.

_____

_____

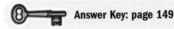 **Answer Key: page 149**

Avoiding Redundancy

A **redundant** sentence is a sentence that repeats information. Look at this sentence.

Sweltering in the heat, the men decided to go inside and cool off where it was cool.

This sentence is poorly written because it says the same thing twice. We already know it was cool inside because the men were going there to cool off. This sentence can be rewritten in two different ways:

©Rolf Brunderer/CORBIS

- Sweltering in the heat, the men decided to go inside and cool off.

- Sweltering in the heat, the men decided to go inside where it was cool.

Important Note

When people speak, they often repeat unnecessary information. That's because they don't have the opportunity to review and edit what they say. When you write, you should always take the time to reread what you have written. As you reread, remember to delete information you have repeated unnecessarily.

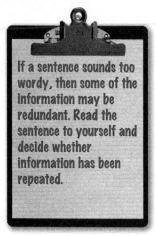

If a sentence sounds too wordy, then some of the information may be redundant. Read the sentence to yourself and decide whether information has been repeated.

Try It

Look at the sentences below and draw a line through information that is redundant and should be deleted.

1. When school was out for the summer, Tyler got a job at the car wash as soon as school was over.

2. Our history homework is due at the beginning of the period on Friday as soon as class begins.

3. Orlando, the captain of the baseball team, headed straight for center field because he was the team captain.

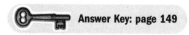 Answer Key: page 149

Combining Sentences

Sometimes you write complete sentences that aren't awkward or redundant but still need to be revised. That's because they contain connected ideas that would make more sense combined. Look at the sentences below.

> 1. Alex looked out the window at the snow-covered ground.
> 2. He knew that today's game would be canceled because of snow.

These sentences are complete, but they sound choppy. Here is one way to combine them:

> Looking out the window at the snow-covered ground, Alex knew that today's game would be canceled.

The subjects in sentences 1 and 2 (*Alex* and *He*) have been combined into one subject (*Alex*). The predicate in the first sentence has been turned into a participial phrase. Also, a phrase that was redundant (*because of snow*) has been deleted.

Can you think of another way to combine sentences 1 and 2 in the box above? Write your sentence on the lines below.

_____

_____

Parallelism

When you combine sentences in your writing, you need to make sure that the ideas in the new sentence are parallel. This means that the sentence contains the same forms of the subject and verb. Combined sentences that aren't parallel are confusing. Read these sentences.

> Jenna likes to water-ski with her friends. Jogging is also something she likes to do with her friends.

Look at the next sentence. Is this an effective way to combine the sentences from the box?

> Jenna likes to water-ski and jogging with her friends.

The new sentence sounds wrong because the ideas are not parallel. How could you make this sentence parallel? Here are two ways:

> Jenna likes water-skiing and jogging with her friends.
>
> Jenna likes to water-ski and jog with her friends.

There are many different reasons and ways to combine sentences. Look at the examples below. Notice why and how the sentences are combined. The best way to combine the sentences in each box is marked with a ✓.

> ### A Subject Is Repeated
>
> **Choppy:** Eating at restaurants is fun. Eating at restaurants is easy. Eating at restaurants can be expensive.
>
> **Combined but redundant and a run-on:** Eating at restaurants is fun and easy, eating at restaurants can also be expensive.
>
> ✓ **Combined and parallel:** Eating at restaurants is fun and easy, but it can also be expensive.

Words Are Repeated

Choppy: The mongoose slipped quietly into the cobra's hole. At the same time the cobra slithered out the other side of its hole.

Combined but inaccurate: The mongoose slipped quietly into the cobra's hole since the cobra slithered out the other side of its hole.

✓ **Combined and accurate:** As the mongoose slipped quietly into the cobra's hole, the cobra slithered out the other side.

Something Changes Between Sentences

Choppy: An elaborate sand castle stands proudly near the dunes. The sand castle is washed away by the tide.

Combined but wordy: An elaborate sand castle stands proudly near the dunes until the sand castle is washed away by the tide.

✓ **Combined and less wordy:** An elaborate sand castle stands proudly near the dunes until it is washed away by the tide.

Something Makes Another Thing Happen

Choppy: I missed the bus. My father picked me up after practice.

Combined but awkward: I missed the bus after practice that my father picked me up from.

✓ **Combined and clear:** I missed the bus, so my father picked me up after practice.

Something Happens Before Something Else

Choppy: Ryan can apply for a job as a lifeguard. He has to take a lifesaving course first.

Combined but unparallel: Before Ryan can apply for a job as a lifeguard, a lifesaving course has to be taken.

✓ **Combined and parallel:** Before Ryan can apply for a job as a lifeguard, he has to take a lifesaving course.

Try It

Now look at the sentences below. Combine the sentences on the lines provided.

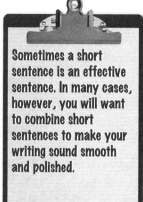

Sometimes a short sentence is an effective sentence. In many cases, however, you will want to combine short sentences to make your writing sound smooth and polished.

1. Maria wrote a short story. It was about a family that immigrated to this country in the 1800s.

_____

_____

_____

2. Riley applied for a job. The store manager told him that he needed more experience.

_____

_____

_____

3. Jessie was running for home plate. She slipped and scraped her knee.

_____

_____

_____

4. I worked at my dad's office all summer. I saved enough money to buy a new computer.

_____

_____

_____

5. Felicia and Sam ate lunch at Ratliff Park. They played basketball at the park, too.

_____

_____

_____

Answer Key: page 149

Standard English Usage

Imagine you are at a restaurant and have ordered a delicious dish of grilled fish. When your meal is served, you receive a steaming plate of macaroni and cheese instead. It may still be food, but it's not what you ordered. A similar thing happens when you write without following the rules of standard English. You may still be writing sentences, but they don't accurately convey your message.

Important Note

Following the rules of standard English will ensure that your writing is as clear and precise as it can be. Readers will be more likely to understand the ideas you are expressing.

Subject-Verb Agreement

Remember that every sentence must have a subject and a verb. Subjects and verbs must agree in number. This means that when you have a singular subject, you must have a singular verb. Plural subjects require plural verbs.

Look at the sentences below.

Delbert **rides** the bus to school on Fridays.

Caleb, Shelly, and Simone **ride** the bus to school every day.

The first sentence has a singular subject (*Delbert*) and a singular verb (*rides*). This singular verb ends in *-s*, which is true of many singular verbs. The second sentence has a plural subject (*Caleb, Shelly, and Simone*) and a plural verb (*ride*).

Study the singular and plural subjects and verbs below.

A singular subject always takes a singular verb.	<u>Nathan</u> <u>is</u> my friend.
A plural subject always takes a plural verb.	<u>Nathan and Brad</u> <u>are</u> my friends.
A singular pronoun always takes a singular verb.	<u>Each</u> of the boys <u>runs</u> track.
A subject and a verb always agree, regardless of what comes between them.	<u>The coach</u>, tired from working so many long nights, <u>wasn't</u> at school today.
A subject and a verb always agree, even if the verb comes before the subject in the sentence.	In the classroom <u>are</u> two new <u>students</u>.

Try It

Read the sentences below and think about subject-verb agreement. Fill in each blank with the correct verb form.

1. Earth _____ on its axis once every 24 hours.
   (rotate, rotates)

2. Writing in a journal _____ a calming effect on Steve.   (has, have)

3. Tree leaves _____ color as the weather turns colder.   (change, changes)

4. Danielle and Scott _____ together to make dinner.   (work, works)

5. Taking a walk with my neighbors _____ me for the rest of the night.   (refresh, refreshes)

Answer Key: page 149

117

Verb Tense

Verb **tense** tells when the action in a sentence takes place.

Tense	When	Example
Present	Now	Jason **washes** his car.
Past	Before now	Jason **washed** his car yesterday.
Future	After now	Jason **will wash** his car tomorrow.

The past tense of a verb is usually formed by adding *-ed*, but some verbs are different. These are called **irregular** verbs. Here are some examples of irregular verbs:

Verb	Past Tense
drink	drank
write	wrote
throw	threw

Try It

Some writers make mistakes because they use incorrect past-tense forms of verbs. Look at the following paragraph. Circle any verbs that have not been formed correctly.

> Yesterday we **waked** up, **eated** breakfast, and **drived** straight to the bus station. My art class **was meeting** at the art museum downtown. Our teacher **wanted** to show us some great artists' masterpieces. After viewing the remarkable art, we **returned** to school and **maked** paintings of our own. They **have hanged** in the school hallway ever since.

What are the correct forms of the verbs you circled? Write them on the lines below.

_____

_____

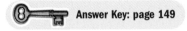 Answer Key: page 149

Faulty Tense Shifts

When we talk, we may shift from one tense to another without confusing our listeners. When we write, however, changing from one tense to another can cause a lot of confusion. Read the sentences in the box.

> Yesterday Kylie comes by the house after she ran at the track. She is working hard every day because she had wanted to make the track team. "Are you ready for tryouts?" I asked.
>
> She shook her head and smiles at me. "Not quite," she answers, "but I am by the end of next week."

Can you count the number of times the tense shifts in the sentences above? In the first sentence *Yesterday* signals past tense, but it is followed by the present-tense verb *comes*. Then the writer shifts between present and past tense in the next four sentences. In the last sentence the writer is talking about something that will happen next week, but she writes in the present tense.

When you write, you should shift tenses only if you have a good reason to do so. Here is the same paragraph written correctly:

> Yesterday Kylie **came** by the house after she ran at the track. She **has been** working hard every day because she **wants** to make the track team. "Are you ready for tryouts?" I asked.
>
> She shook her head and **smiled** at me. "Not quite," she **answered**, "but I **will be** by the end of next week."

Because this event happened in the past, most of the paragraph is now in the past tense. The verb *wants* is in the present tense because making the track team is an ongoing desire that Kylie has. The verb *will be* is in the future tense because this sentence is talking about something that will happen in the future.

Try It

Read these sentences. Circle the verb form that will make the verb tenses in each sentence consistent.

1. At the basketball game I **buy/bought** popcorn and shared it with my cousin.

2. Mitch and Rosa left the canoe on the bank and **swam/had swum** across the stream.

3. The fan in my room is broken and **needed/needs** to be repaired.

4. After school I usually **feed/fed** the dog and load the dishwasher.

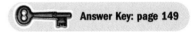 **Answer Key: page 149**

Pronoun-Antecedent Agreement

Just as a verb must agree with its subject, a pronoun must agree with the noun it is replacing. A **pronoun** is a word used in place of a noun. Some examples of pronouns are *I, she, him, we, myself,* and *your.* The number and gender of the pronoun depend on its **antecedent**, or the noun it is replacing.

Look at this sentence.

> After the **buyer** purchased the set of dishes, **they** noticed a chip in one of the plates.

This sentence is incorrect because the pronoun and its antecedent do not agree in number. There is only one buyer, but the pronoun *they* stands for more than one person.

Now look at this sentence.

> **Mr. Myers** delivered the package at the last stop on **her** route.

This sentence is incorrect because the pronoun and its antecedent do not agree in gender. Mr. Myers is a male, but the pronoun *her* refers to a female.

Pronoun Case

When you use pronouns, you must also be sure to use them in the correct **case**, or form. For example, when you're talking about yourself, there are five different pronouns you can use in four different cases.

I	Nominative case—used as the subject
me	Objective case—used as the direct object, indirect object, or object of a preposition
my, mine	Possessive case—used to show ownership
myself	Reflexive case—used to refer back to the subject of a verb or to add emphasis

> **I** am getting a puppy for **my** grandmother today. **My** dad will help **my** brother and **me** build a fence in Grandma's yard. The dog won't be **mine**, but I will help Grandma take care of it.

In these sentences the writer uses four different pronouns to refer to himself, but each pronoun is used correctly. That's because the pronouns are used in different ways in the sentences. Therefore, different cases are required.

Now look at this sentence.

> Jester and Delilah had a surprise for my twin sister and I.

This sentence sounds very formal, and some people would say it is correct. However, look at the pronoun *I*. Is it used as the subject? No. It's the object of the preposition *for*, so *I* is not the correct pronoun to use. The sentence should read as follows:

> Jester and Delilah had a surprise for my twin sister and **me**.

> ### Important Note
> When you have a noun and a pronoun used in the same way in a sentence, taking out the noun and leaving just the pronoun can sometimes help you decide which case the pronoun should take. For example, *Jester and Delilah had a surprise for ~~my twin sister and~~ me.*

Try It

Think about what you have reviewed regarding pronoun-antecedent agreement and pronoun case. Select the correct pronoun for each sentence below.

1. It is important for students to return to **their/them** seats before Mrs. Taylor gets here.

2. The class will discuss international law and **their/its** relevance in today's world.

3. A note taker will record the opinions that are expressed, and **it/they** will be compiled into a document for everyone to read.

4. Students will form teams so that **we/they** can analyze the information and draw conclusions about **them/it**.

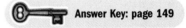 Answer Key: page 149

Clear Pronoun Reference

Sometimes a reader may be unsure which noun or noun phrase a pronoun is meant to replace. Look at the sentence below.

©Paul Barton/CORBIS

> Buying a car requires saving money and comparing prices. **It** can be scary without guidance.

What does the pronoun *it* in the second sentence refer to?

- Buying a car?

- Saving money?

- Comparing prices?

This sentence is confusing because the pronoun *it* could refer to three different noun phrases. How can you rewrite this sentence to make its meaning clearer? It depends on what the writer is trying to say, but here are a couple of ways the sentence can be rewritten:

- Buying a car requires saving money and comparing prices. This important purchase can be scary without guidance.

- Buying a car requires saving money and comparing prices. Without guidance, all these things can be scary.

Double Indicators

Remember that a pronoun is used only in place of a noun, not in addition to a noun. Writers sometimes confuse their readers by using pronouns when they are not necessary. Look at the sentence below.

> Jamal and Justine they were late to school yesterday.

What nouns does the pronoun *they* refer to in this sentence? It refers to *Jamal and Justine*, but because it comes right after their names, this pronoun isn't necessary. To clarify this sentence, you need to delete either the names or the pronoun.

Correct Word Choice

When you write, you must also be careful to choose the correct words. Some words sound almost the same but have different spellings and meanings. Here are some examples:

then/than	except/accept	formally/formerly
are/our	loose/lose	quiet/quite

Homonyms are words that sound exactly alike but have different spellings and meanings. Here are some common homonyms:

your/you're	right/write	principal/principle
two/too/to	board/bored	piece/peace
there/their/they're	who's/whose	waste/waist

Try It

Look at these sentences.

Its important to choose a coarse of study that interests you when your planning you're future. Otherwise you may get board and loose focus in the years ahead.

Can you identify places where incorrect words have been used in these sentences? Rewrite the sentences correctly on the lines below.

_____

_____

_____

_____

Answer Key: page 149

Informal Language

Sometimes you might write a sentence that sounds correct but isn't clear. This often occurs when people write as they would speak.

You might say: The newspaper guy wrote a whole bunch of stuff about how the city's traffic is messed up.

You should write: The newspaper reporter wrote a long article about the city's traffic problems.

Try It

Write a sentence you would say if you were talking to your friends. Then write the same idea in the way you would need to write it in a composition for school. Note the differences.

_____

_____

_____

_____

Confusing Parts of Speech

Choosing the right word to use also depends on what the word will be doing in the sentence. Will it serve as a noun, a verb, an adjective, or an adverb?

Look at this sentence.

> Before purchasing carpet, you need an exact measured of the room.

How is *measured* being used in this sentence? It is something you need before you can purchase the carpet. Since it is a thing, it needs to be a noun, so *measured* can't be right. *Measured* is a verb. Think about other forms of this word: *measure, measuring, measurement.* Which form would be the best choice for this sentence? *Measurement* is the best choice because it is a noun.

Look at this sentence.

> Mrs. Li's _____ with the new student convinced us that she would be fair.

What kind of word needs to go in the blank? Should it be a noun, a verb, an adjective, an adverb, or a pronoun? We are talking about one of Mrs. Li's qualities, so this blank requires a noun. Which of the following words could go in the blank—*gentle, gently, gentler,* or *gentleness*? The word *gentleness* is a noun, so it is the best choice.

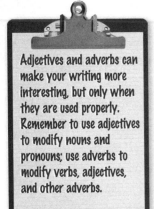

Adjectives and adverbs can make your writing more interesting, but only when they are used properly. Remember to use adjectives to modify nouns and pronouns; use adverbs to modify verbs, adjectives, and other adverbs.

Adjectives Versus Adverbs

What is the difference between an adjective and an adverb? Both words are used to describe, but an adjective describes a noun or a pronoun, while an adverb describes a verb, an adjective, or another adverb. Look at the ways adjectives and adverbs are used in the sentences below.

Adjective	Adverb	How are they used in a sentence?	What modifies what?
deep	very	Brian dug a very deep hole.	*Very* modifies *deep*. *Deep* modifies *hole*.
beautiful	uncommonly	The divers found an uncommonly beautiful stone.	*Uncommonly* modifies *beautiful*. *Beautiful* modifies *stone*.
patient	usually	He usually tries to be a patient person.	*Usually* modifies *tries*. *Patient* modifies *person*.
courteous	quietly	The courteous guest quietly entered the room.	*Courteous* modifies *guest*. *Quietly* modifies *entered*.
brave	cautiously	The brave firefighter cautiously lowered the ladder.	*Brave* modifies *firefighter*. *Cautiously* modifies *lowered*.

Try It

Look at the sentences below. Decide whether each blank needs an adjective or an adverb. Then write the correct word in the blank.

1. With his _____ study complete, Hyram was
   (independent, independently)

   finally able to relax.

2. Skating _____ across the ice, Dana began
   (graceful, gracefully)

   her routine.

3. Looking forward to a new year, Elliot _____
   (eager, eagerly)

   joined the debate team.

Answer Key: page 149

Mechanics

When you express your ideas in writing, it is important to use not only the appropriate words, phrases, and sentences, but also the correct mechanics of standard English. Mechanics include punctuation, capitalization, and spelling. Applying these skills correctly will help your readers understand what you are trying to communicate.

Punctuation

Punctuation refers to the marks writers use to show readers when a sentence ends, how a sentence should be read, when a pause is necessary, and when a person is speaking. Correct punctuation guides a reader through a piece of writing. Incorrect punctuation, on the other hand, can cause great confusion.

End Punctuation

Every sentence must end with some form of punctuation.

- A **statement** ends with a period. (*Last night's homecoming game had to be postponed because of lightning.*)

- An **exclamatory** sentence ends with an exclamation point. (*Watching the meteor shower from Deborah's balcony was absolutely breathtaking!*)

- A direct **question** ends with a question mark. (*Where will Brian work when the construction project on Baker Street is finished?*)

Commas

Commas separate items and help readers know when to pause. Commas can be used

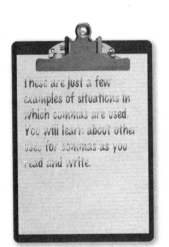

- to set off quotation marks (*The teacher stressed, "Review your papers carefully before you turn them in."*)

- between items in a series (*The vendors at the game served grilled hot dogs, roasted corn, and bottled water.*)

- between independent clauses joined by a coordinating conjunction (such as *and*, *but*, and *or*) in a compound sentence (*Pauline wrote an essay, but she forgot to turn the assignment in.*)

- between coordinate adjectives (*Jessie lay in her hammock under the glowing, gigantic moon.*)

- to separate nonessential clauses (*I opened the window, which had been closed last night, to let in a light breeze.*)

- after nonrestrictive appositives (*Kylie, the woman who lives in the apartment next door to us, knew how to fix our leaky faucet.*)

- after an introductory participial phrase (*Returning home from the county fair, Jed and Billy decided to take an unusual shortcut.*)

- after an introductory subordinate clause (*Because I'm interested in astronomy, I'm thinking of visiting Johnson Space Center in Houston.*)

- to set off a city and state (*We lived in Dallas, Texas, for two years.*)

- to set off a date and year (*My internship begins on August 23, 2003, and continues for six months.*)

Semicolons, Colons, and Apostrophes

Semicolons and colons are not used as often as commas, but they are still important. Semicolons are used to

- separate parts of a compound sentence when no conjunction is used (*Darren looked into the catfish bucket; he couldn't believe the size of the fish he had caught.*)

- separate items in a series that already contains commas (*The debate club decided that it would hold meetings on January 10, 2003; February 2, 2004; January 18, 2005; and February 6, 2006.*)

Colons are used

- to set off an explanation or example that follows an independent clause (*There are eight planets in our solar system: Mercury, Venus, Earth, Mars, Jupiter, Saturn, Neptune, and Uranus.*)

- in time descriptions (*The school bell always rang at exactly 3:30 in the afternoon.*)

Apostrophes are used to

- show possession (*Link's hamster could run much faster than Huang's turtle.*)

- create contractions (*The mall isn't open until noon on Sundays.*)

Try It

Look at the paragraph below. Where are commas, semicolons, colons, and apostrophes needed? Insert the proper punctuation marks.

In Yuma Arizona todays high temperature was 109 degrees four degrees above normal. Temperatures have been equally uncomfortable all week 103 degrees 104 degrees 100 degrees and 105 degrees. One local businessman said Wed move to Phoenix but the weather isnt much cooler there. For Yuma residents the news doesnt get any better next week no rain is expected until Saturday.

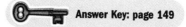 **Answer Key: page 149**

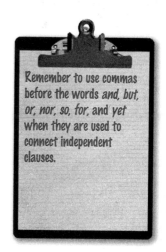

Remember to use commas before the words *and, but, or, nor, so, for,* and *yet* when they are used to connect independent clauses.

Quotation Marks

Quotation marks (" ") are used within a piece of writing to show that a person is speaking. When you use quotation marks, you must follow certain punctuation and capitalization rules. Look at the quotation marks in the sentences below. Pay attention to the punctuation and capitalization.

> Julia remarked, "The drama club is hosting a picnic at Taylor Field on Saturday."
>
> "Who's invited?" Tad quickly asked.
>
> "You and your buddies are welcome," Sandra responded, "if you don't mind bringing the soft drinks."

Look at the first sentence. When the speaker is identified before the quotation, a comma is used before the opening quotation marks. The first word of the quotation is capitalized. Correct end punctuation is used before the closing quotation marks.

Now look at the second sentence. When a quotation comes before the speaker is identified, the first word of the quote is still capitalized. A comma, question mark, or exclamation point is used before the closing quotation marks. Then a period is used at the end of the sentence.

Now look at the third sentence. This sentence is a little different. Part of the quotation comes before the speaker is identified, and part comes after. The first word of the quotation is capitalized, and a comma is used before the first closing quotation marks. Then another comma is used before the second opening quotation marks. Since the rest of the quote is still part of the sentence, a capital letter is not used when the quote is reopened. Correct end punctuation is used at the end of this sentence, just before the second closing quotation marks.

Try It

Think about what you have learned. Rewrite the sentences below, using quotation marks and correct end punctuation.

1. Hyacinth said Go across the street and stand under that lamp

   _____

2. Are you planning to attend the family reunion his cousin asked

   _____

3. Look out the policeman shouted I see another tornado coming in from the east

   _____

   _____

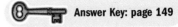 Answer Key: page 149

Capitalization

Some words in the English language need to begin with a capital letter. You know to capitalize the first word in a sentence, and you just reviewed capitalizing the first word in a direct quotation. Proper nouns and proper adjectives are other words that must begin with capital letters.

- Proper nouns name specific people, places, and things (*Mount Rushmore, the Dead Sea, the White House, South Dakota*).

- Proper adjectives are adjectives that are formed from proper nouns (*the French countryside, English literature, Italian dressing*).

If you can learn to recognize proper nouns, proper adjectives will be easy to identify, too. Look at the chart below.

Common Noun	Proper Noun	Proper Adjective (with a noun it might modify)
country	Brazil	Brazilian coffee
country	England	English tea
continent	Africa	African music

Try It

Read the paragraph below. Circle the proper nouns and proper adjectives that need to be capitalized.

On a recent trip to houston, lisa ate pizza in an italian restaurant. Then she met her friend sue at the mall on west street. While there, she bought some french perfume as a gift for her mother. Before leaving the mall, the girls entered a contest to win a european vacation. Lisa decided that the trip to houston was even more fun than her trip to the beach last year.

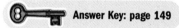 **Answer Key: page 149**

Spelling

It is important to spell words correctly so that readers will know what you are trying to say. The chart below shows some rules to help you spell English words.

Rule	Examples
When a word ends in a short vowel followed by one consonant, double the consonant before adding a suffix that starts with a vowel.	compel + -*ing* = compelling split + -*ing* = splitting snap + -*ing* = snapping
When a word ends in a silent -*e*, drop the -*e* before adding a suffix that starts with a vowel.	inhale + -*ing* = inhaling assure + -*ance* = assurance trudge + -*ed* = trudged
When a word ends in -*y*, change the -*y* to -*i* before adding a suffix that starts with a vowel.	victory + -*ous* = victorious slippery + -*est* = slipperiest supply + -*ed* = supplied
When a word contains the letters *i* and *e* together, the rule is "*i* before *e*, except after *c* or when sounding like '*a*', as in *neighbor* and *weigh*."	thief, chief (*i* before *e*) deceive, ceiling (after *c*, so it's *ei*) sleigh, reign (sounds like "*a*," so it's *ei*)

Sight Words

For many English words there are no spelling rules to help you. You simply have to practice and remember the letter patterns in these words. Here are some examples:

character	dialogue	assignment	knowledge	occasionally
thorough	separate	exaggerate	proportion	medieval

Important Note

When you are unsure of a word's spelling, use a dictionary to double-check. The more times you see and write a word correctly, the more likely you are to eventually remember it. Remember, however, you will not be able to use a dictionary on the revising and editing section of the Grade 10 TAKS ELA test.

Using the Skills

Revising and Editing a Paper

Now that you have reviewed the concepts that must be considered when you are trying to improve the clarity and effectiveness of a piece of writing, you are ready to help a fellow student revise and edit his paper.

The paper on the next two pages was written by a 10th grader named Alex. Read Alex's paper and ask yourself these questions:

- **How well has Alex organized his paper?** Do his ideas flow logically from one to the next? Does he need to include additional details to support any of his ideas? Does he need to add transition words or phrases to connect any of his ideas? Does he need to remove any extraneous sentences?

- **Are Alex's sentences clear and complete?** Does the paper contain any fragments or run-ons? Are any of Alex's sentences awkward or redundant? Are there places where Alex needs to combine ideas?

- **Has Alex followed the rules of standard English?** Does each verb agree with its subject? Are his verbs in the correct tense? Has he used homonyms and pronouns correctly? Does he have any double negatives in the paper?

- **Has Alex made punctuation, capitalization, or spelling errors?** Does each sentence, proper noun, proper adjective, and direct quotation start with a capital letter? Are his commas, semicolons, colons, apostrophes, and quotation marks used correctly? Are all his words spelled correctly?

As you read Alex's paper, you may come to some words or sentences that you think he should change. When this happens, write notes in the margin to tell what is wrong and how you would fix it. When you are finished, look at pages 136–139.

My Invisible Summer

(1) When my application for an internship at the local hard-rock radio station was excepted, I was overjoyed. (2) My friends would be flipping burgers at a fast-food restaurant all summer, but I was going to be a disc jockey, a real DJ. (3) I would use my best DJ voice I would be admired by millions of fans. (4) In no time I would be on my way to fame and fortune.

(5) It didn't take me long to learn that working in radio was not exactly the way I had pictured it. (6) In the movies, radio stations are always situated in gigantic impressive structures in the middle of bustling cities. (7) The radio station where I worked was located in a lonely-looking building on the edge of town. (8) Only the 361-foot antenna made it look at all unusual. (9) The boss explained that the large antenna was necesary for broadcasting at 680,000 megahertz. (10) I tried to look interested as she explained frequency and other electrical terms, but all I really wanted to do was meet the DJs.

(11) I was finally introduced to the DJs I had idolized for years. (12) I was shocked. (13) For some reason I had pictured DJ Kirk Krimson as the kind of person who might star in an action movie, but he didn't look much like a motion-picture star. (14) He told me that when he began in radio, disc jockeys played music on vinyl records, not on compact discs; that really made him seem old.

(15) I didn't have much chance to be disappointed in my DJ heroes, though, because I almost never saw him. (16) My job was to run the station from midnight to 6:00 A.M., and all the DJs worked

during the day. (17) They recorded their shows, and I just played tapes of their voices and song choices. (18) Between tapes I plugged in recorded commercials. (19) My favorite commercial was one about a new video game. (20) Three times a night I got to talk on the air for 10 seconds—but only to read the call letters, the four-letter name that the Federal Communications Commission had assigned to the station. (21) I never even got to say my own name! (22) Maybe I'll try flipping burgers next summer.

How Should Alex Revise His Paper?

Sentence 1

Did you find anything that you wanted to change in sentence 1? Look again at the sentence.

When my application for an internship at the local hard-rock radio station was excepted, I was overjoyed.

Did Alex use correct words in this sentence? Look at the word *excepted*. Is this what Alex meant to say? No. *Excepted* comes from the word *except*, which means "to leave out or exclude someone or something." That's not what Alex is trying to say. The word Alex is trying to use is the word **accepted**. Alex needs to change this word.

Sentence 3

What about sentence 3? Did you mark anything here? Read the sentence again.

I would use my best DJ voice I would be admired by millions of fans.

The sentence is a run-on. There is nothing to connect or separate the two complete sentences. What would be the most effective way to correct this run-on?

- *I would use my best DJ voice, I would be admired by millions of fans.*
- *I would use my best DJ voice, which is admired by millions of fans.*
- *I would use my best DJ voice and be admired by millions of fans.*

The first choice is incorrect because just adding a comma doesn't correct a run-on. This is still two sentences without the proper punctuation or capitalization.

The second choice is incorrect because the meaning of the original second sentence has been changed. The original sentence doesn't say that the writer's DJ voice *is admired by millions of fans*. The sentence says that the writer himself *would be admired by millions of fans*.

The third choice is correct. The word *and* is used to connect the two sentences. To avoid redundancy, the subject *I* and verb *would* are used only once.

Sentence 6

Did you notice a mechanics error in sentence 6? Study the sentence again.

> *In the movies, radio stations are always situated in gigantic impressive structures in the middle of bustling cities.*

Is there a capitalization mistake? Is a word misspelled? Is a punctuation mark missing?

Look at the words *gigantic impressive*. These are coordinate adjectives. Both words are modifying the word *structures*, and they are equally important. A comma should be used to separate coordinate adjectives. The sentence should read as follows:

> *In the movies, radio stations are always situated in gigantic, impressive structures in the middle of bustling cities.*

Sentence 9

What about this sentence? What is wrong here?

> *The boss explained that the large antenna was **necesary** for broadcasting at 680,000 megahertz.*

Do any of the words in this sentence look odd to you? Look again at the boldfaced word. Is it spelled correctly? It doesn't look right, does it? *Necessary* is the correct way to spell this word.

Sentences 11 and 12

What did you think about these two sentences?

> *I was finally introduced to the DJs I had idolized for years. I was shocked.*

Both sentences are grammatically correct, but the second sentence sounds a little choppy. How can you combine sentences 11 and 12?

- *When I was finally introduced to the DJs I had idolized for years, I was shocked.*

- *Finally introduced to the DJs I had idolized and shocked for years.*

- *I was finally introduced to the DJs I had idolized for years, I was shocked.*

The first choice is a clear and complete sentence. *When* connects the two ideas, and it seems like an appropriate connection. Let's read the other two choices to be sure this is the best one.

The second choice can't be right. It's a fragment, and it's also inaccurate. The writer had idolized the DJs for years, but he hadn't shocked them.

The third choice is incorrect because the two sentences were put together with only a comma between them. Two sentences cannot be combined just by putting a comma between them. That will always create a run-on.

The first choice is the best way to combine sentences 11 and 12.

Sentence 13

There's nothing wrong with sentence 13, but what if you wanted to add a little more detail to develop this idea further? Which of these ideas could logically follow sentence 13?

- *He had worked nights at a warehouse when he was younger.*

- *Later I saw a picture of him on the wall in the hallway.*

- *He looked more like a friend that my dad would bring home.*

Think about sentence 13. Alex wrote that Kirk Krimson didn't look much like a motion-picture star. If Alex wanted to develop this idea further, what would he need to write more about? He'd need to write more about what Kirk Krimson looked like.

Look at the first two choices. The facts that Kirk Krimson worked at a warehouse and that his picture was in the hallway don't tell anything more about how he looked. The third choice says that he looked like a friend the writer's father would bring home. That tells more about what Kirk Krimson looked like, so the third idea is the one that could logically follow sentence 13.

Sentence 15

Did you find a mistake in sentence 15? If not, read the sentence again.

> *I didn't have much chance to be disappointed in my DJ heroes, though, because I almost never saw him.*

Does this sentence sound right? Did Alex follow the rules of standard English? Look at the pronoun *him*. What noun does this pronoun refer to? Whom did the writer almost never see? The writer is talking about his *DJ heroes*, but *him* is a singular pronoun. It can refer to only one person. The writer needs a plural pronoun to refer to the noun *heroes*. This is how the sentence should read:

> *I didn't have much chance to be disappointed in my DJ heroes, though, because I almost never saw **them**.*

Sentence 19

Did anything seem odd about this sentence? Read the last paragraph again and pay careful attention to sentence 19.

What did you notice? Did you identify sentence 19 as an extraneous sentence? This sentence should be deleted because it does not fit in the logical progression of the paragraph. This paragraph is about what the writer did during his shift on the radio. Even though he mentions the fact that he played recorded commercials during his shift, the writer's favorite commercial is not important.

How Does TAKS Test the Skills You Have Been Reviewing?

On the English Language Arts (ELA) test, you will be asked to review some passages created to look like student writing. The passages will contain mistakes. You will need to study the passages and decide how each one should be corrected and improved. Remember, you will not be able to use a dictionary on this part of the test.

The passages on the following pages are like the ones you will see on a real TAKS test. As you read each passage, think about what needs to be changed.

Important Note

● Read the first passage and think about how you would correct and improve it.

● Look at the first question and the corresponding answer choices. Decide which answer choice is correct and mark it. Read the rest of the questions and mark an answer for each one.

● Look at pages 150–151 of the Answer Key. Compare your answers to the answers given there. Read the explanation next to each answer choice. These explanations will help you understand why one choice is correct and the others are not.

● Read the second passage and answer the corresponding questions.

● Return to the Answer Key and look at pages 151–153. Compare your answers to the answers given there.

©Mug Shots/CORBIS

Revising and Editing: Practice Passage 1 and Questions

Tanisha has written this story for a creative writing assignment. As part of a peer-editing conference, you have been asked to read the story and think about the changes you would make. When you finish reading, answer the questions that follow.

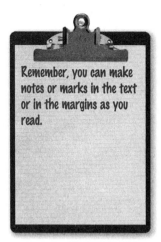

Remember, you can make notes or marks in the text or in the margins as you read.

Star Party

(1) The sun was just beginning to set as members of the Washington High School astronomy club climbed out of the van in front of the visitors' information center. (2) The rugged peaks surounding them seemed to be from another planet. (3) The students were accustomed to the flat southeast Texas landscape that they had left the day before. (4) Soon, for example, they would be seeing real planets at their own private star party. (5) They were excited to be at the McDonald Observatory in the mountains of West Texas, which is perched on a summit.

(6) Steve, a volunteer staff member, greeted the students and their sponsors. (7) He began the program by pointing out the planets, stars, and constellations that can be seen by the naked eye. (8) He used a bright flashlight. (9) One group of stars were especially brilliant that evening.

(10) "This is one of the best spots in North America for an observatory," Steve told the group. (11) "Astronomers from all over the world come to use our telescope. (12) We're at an altitude of nearly 7,000 feet, and the nearest large city is about 150 miles away, making the night sky here more dark than in almost any other place in the United States. (13) In this climate the night sky doesn't get its view distorted by moisture in the air because the air contains little of it. (14) In addition, we are located close enough to the equator to view many astronomical objects that can't be seen farther north.

(15) So you can see why our observatory is such an excellent place for star parties.

(16) Then came the best part of the star party. (17) Aided by Steve and other volunteers, they peered through several telescopes for a closer look at the stars and planets. (18) Exclamations of surprise and wonder echoed throughout the room. (19) Many students said that it was almost like being in outer space. (20) This was the first time the club had visited this observatory. (21) On the way back to their lodging in nearby Fort Davis, the club members decided to call themselves the Mountain Astronauts.

Question 1

What change, if any, should be made in sentence 2?

A Change *peaks* to *peeks*

B Change *surounding* to *surrounding*

C Insert a comma after *them*

D Make no change

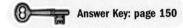 Answer Key: page 150

Question 2

What transition should replace *for example* in sentence 4?

A however

B consequently

C therefore

D nevertheless

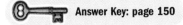 Answer Key: page 150

Question 3

What revision, if any, should be made in sentence 5?

A They were excited to be at the McDonald Observatory in the mountains of West Texas. Which is perched on a summit.

B They were excited to be at the McDonald Observatory in the mountains of West Texas, it is perched on a summit.

C They were excited to be at the McDonald Observatory, which is perched on a summit in the mountains of West Texas.

D No revision is needed.

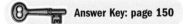 Answer Key: page 150

Question 4

What is the most effective way to combine sentences 7 and 8?

A He began the program by pointing out the planets, stars, and constellations with a bright flashlight that can be seen by the naked eye.

B He began the program and used a bright flashlight and pointed out the planets, stars, and constellations that can be seen by the naked eye.

C He began the program by pointing out the planets, stars, and constellations that can be seen by the naked eye, he used a bright flashlight.

D He began the program by using a bright flashlight to point out the planets, stars, and constellations that can be seen by the naked eye.

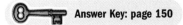 Answer Key: page 150

Question 5

What change, if any, should be made in sentence 9?

A Insert **they** after *stars*

B Change *were* to **was**

C Change *especially* to **especialy**

D Make no change

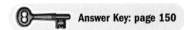 Answer Key: page 150

Question 6

What change should be made in sentence 12?

A Change *We're* to **Were**

B Delete the comma after *away*

C Change *more dark* to **darker**

D Change *than* to **then**

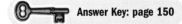 Answer Key: page 150

Question 7

What is the most effective way to rewrite the ideas in sentence 13?

A In this climate the night sky doesn't get its view distorted by moisture in the air, the air contains little of it.

B The air in this climate contains little moisture to distort the view of the night sky.

C Because the air in this climate contains little moisture. It doesn't distort the view of the night sky.

D Containing little moisture, the air in this climate doesn't get its view distorted by the night sky.

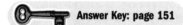 Answer Key: page 151

Question 8

What change, if any, is needed in sentence 15?

A Change *our* to **are**

B Change *is* to **was**

C Insert quotation marks after the period

D Make no change

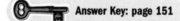 Answer Key: page 151

Question 9

The meaning of sentence 17 can be clarified by changing *they* to —

A we

B the volunteers

C Steve

D the members of the astronomy club

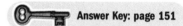 Answer Key: page 151

Question 10

What is the most effective way to improve the organization of the last paragraph (sentences 16–21)?

A Delete sentence 16

B Switch sentences 16 and 19

C Delete sentence 20

D Move sentence 21 to follow sentence 16

Answer Key: page 151

Revising and Editing: Practice Passage 2 and Questions

As part of a biology project, Elizabeth wrote this paper about Jane Goodall. She wants you to read the report and suggest how she might correct and improve it. When you have finished reading, answer the questions that follow.

Living with the Chimps

(1) When a little girl was just two years old, her father gave her a toy chimpanzee named Jubilee. (2) The chimp became one of the girl's most treasured possessions. (3) In later years she read books about animals, including *The Story of Dr. Dolittle*, *Tarzan of the Apes*, and *The Jungle Book*. (4) She dreamed of someday living with and to write about animals. (5) That young girl was Jane Goodall, and her dream became a reality. (6) Today Goodall is one of the world's leading primatologists, which means that she may know more about chimpanzees then anyone else on the planet.

(7) In those days a young single woman didn't travel into the jungle, but that didn't stop Goodall. (8) Goodall, who was born in London in 1934, traveled to the banks of Lake Tanganyika in East Africa in 1957. (9) A friend had invited her on the journey, and she was eager to see the wild animals she had read about. (10) Goodall was excited by what she experienced and learned on her trip, she soon realized that she had found her life's work. (11) Three years later she met world-renowned anthropologist and paleontologist Louis Leakey. (12) Leakey hired her as his assistant and gave her the opportunity to help him with an in-depth study of wild chimpanzees.

(13) For the next few decades, Goodall spent her time in the jungle becoming a part of the chimpanzee's lives. (14) She started by observing them from afar through binoculars. (15) As the chimpanzees grew to accept her presence, she moved in closer. (16) She watched

the primates carefully. (17) Recording information about their actions and relationships. (18) She was amazed at the similarities she saw between man and chimpanzee. (19) She made a number of surprising discoveries regarding the animals, including their ability to make and use tools.

(20) During those years Goodall returned from the jungle to earn an advanced degree from Cambridge university. (21) She also established the Gombe Stream Resource Centre and the Jane Goodall Institute, both are dedicated to providing support for chimpanzee research. (22) She wrote many books and articles about her work and campaigned to help protect the natural environment of the chimpanzee. (23) Today Goodall tours the world and talks about her experiences. (24) Each time she returns home, a familiar face is there waiting for her—Jubilee, her oldest companion and the one who may have helped spark her life's passion.

Question 11

What revision, if any, should be made in sentence 4?

A She dreamed of someday living with and writing about animals.

B She dreamed of someday living with animals. To also write about the animals.

C She dreamed of someday living with animals, she wanted to write about them.

D No revision is needed.

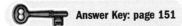 Answer Key: page 151

Question 12

What change, if any, should be made in sentence 6?

A Change *world's* to **worlds'**

B Delete the comma after *primatologists*

C Change *then* to **than**

D Make no change

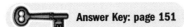 Answer Key: page 151

Question 13

What is the most effective way to improve the organization of the second paragraph (sentences 7–12)?

A Switch sentences 7 and 8

B Delete sentence 11

C Switch sentences 11 and 12

D Move sentence 12 to follow sentence 8

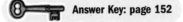 Answer Key: page 152

Question 14

What revision, if any, is needed in sentence 10?

A Goodall was excited by what she experienced and learned on her trip. And soon realized that she had found her life's work.

B Excited by what she experienced and learned on her trip. Goodall soon realized that she had found her life's work.

C Excited by what she experienced and learned on her trip, Goodall soon realized that she had found her life's work.

D No revision is needed.

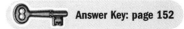 Answer Key: page 152

Question 15

What change, if any, is needed in sentence 13?

A Change *spent* to **spends**

B Change *chimpanzee's* to **chimpanzees'**

C Change *lives* to **lifes**

D Make no change

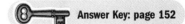 Answer Key: page 152

Question 16

How should sentences 16 and 17 be revised?

A She watched the primates carefully because they were recording information, and it was about their actions and relationships.

B She watched the primates carefully, she recorded information about their actions and relationships.

C She watched the primates carefully, recording information about their actions and relationships.

D No revision is needed.

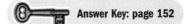 Answer Key: page 152

Question 17

Which of these ideas could best be added after sentence 19?

A Isn't it astonishing that chimpanzees can use tools?

B She was surprised at some of the discoveries she made.

C Tools can be made from many different materials.

D This information changed the way the world viewed primates.

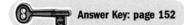 Answer Key: page 152

Question 18

What change, if any, should be made in sentence 20?

A Insert **it was** after *jungle*

B Insert a comma after *degree*

C Change *university* to **University**

D Make no change

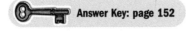 Answer Key: page 152

Question 19

What change, if any, should be made in sentence 21?

A Change *Institute* to **institute**

B Change the comma to a semicolon

C Change *providing* to **provideing**

D Make no change

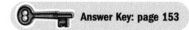 Answer Key: page 153

Question 20

What change, if any, should be made in sentence 24?

A Change *familiar* to **familar**

B Change *there* to **their**

C Change *and* to **it is**

D Make no change

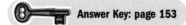 Answer Key: page 153

Revising and Editing Answer Key

Page 109

Possible Answers:

1. We went to the park to watch the play. The performance was to begin at dark.

3. Max stared blankly at the crowd because he had forgotten his lines.

5. I think I'll try out for a part next year; being onstage looked like fun.

Page 111

Shivering under their covers, Lina and her sister heard the howl of the wolf.

Page 112

Possible Answers:

1. Delete the clause *as soon as school was over*.

2. Delete the clause *as soon as class begins*.

3. Delete the clause *because he was the team captain*.

Page 115

Possible Answers:

1. Maria wrote a short story about a family that immigrated to this country in the 1800s.

2. When Riley applied for a job, the store manager told him that he needed more experience.

3. Running for home plate, Jessie slipped and scraped her knee.

4. By working at my dad's office all summer, I saved enough money to buy a new computer.

5. Felicia and Sam ate lunch and played basketball at Ratliff Park.

Page 117

rotates, has, change, work, refreshes

Page 118

Incorrect verb forms: waked, eated, drived, maked, have hanged

Correct verb forms: woke, ate, drove, made, have hung

Page 120

bought, swam, needs, feed

Page 122

their, its, they, they, it

Page 124

It's important to choose a course of study that interests you when you're planning your future. Otherwise you may get bored and lose focus in the years ahead.

Page 126

independent, gracefully, eagerly

Page 129

In Yuma, Arizona, today's high temperature was 109 degrees, four degrees above normal. Temperatures have been equally uncomfortable all week: 103 degrees, 104 degrees, 100 degrees, and 105 degrees. One local businessman said, "We'd move to Phoenix, but the weather isn't much cooler there." For Yuma residents the news doesn't get any better next week; no rain is expected until Saturday.

Page 130

1. Hyacinth said, "Go across the street and stand under that lamp."

2. "Are you planning to attend the family reunion?" his cousin asked.

3. "Look out!" the policeman shouted. "I see another tornado coming in from the east!"

Page 131

On a recent trip to **Houston**, **Lisa** ate pizza in an **Italian** restaurant. Then she met her friend **Sue** at the mall on **West Street**. While there, she bought some **French** perfume as a gift for her mother. Before leaving the mall, the girls entered a contest to win a **European** vacation. Lisa decided that the trip to **Houston** was even more fun than her trip to the beach last year.

"Star Party"

Question 1 (page 143)

Spelling

A Incorrect. The word *peak* is used to refer to the pointed summit of a mountain. The word *peek* means "to take a quick look at something."

B Correct. The word *surounding* needs two *r*'s.

C Incorrect. There is no reason to insert a comma here.

D Incorrect. This sentence contains a spelling mistake.

Question 2 (page 143)

Transition

A Correct. This transition shows a contrast between what they were seeing upon their arrival and what they would be seeing very soon.

B Incorrect. This transition suggests that something was happening as a result of something else.

C Incorrect. This transition also suggests a cause-and-effect relationship that has not been established.

D Incorrect. This transition suggests that one thing happens in spite of another, but no relationship of this kind has been described.

Question 3 (page 143)

Misplaced Modifier

A Incorrect. This answer choice contains a sentence fragment (*Which is perched on a summit*).

B Incorrect. This answer choice is a run-on sentence because it is two complete sentences separated by only a comma.

C Correct. This answer choice is a clear, complete sentence.

D Incorrect. This sentence needs to be revised because it contains a misplaced modifier. The phrase *which is perched on a summit* incorrectly modifies the noun *West Texas*.

Question 4 (page 143)

Sentence Combining

A Incorrect. This answer choice is awkward and inaccurate. It says that the bright flashlight can be seen by the naked eye, which wasn't the intended meaning.

B Incorrect. This answer choice is redundant because it says Steve *began the program and used a bright flashlight and pointed out the planets*. An effective sentence does not use only the word *and* to connect a series of ideas.

C Incorrect. This answer choice is a run-on sentence because it is two complete sentences separated by only a comma.

D Correct. This answer choice is a clear, complete sentence that accurately reflects the information given in the two original sentences.

Question 5 (page 143)

Subject-Verb Agreement

A Incorrect. There is no reason to add a pronoun right after the noun it refers to. This would be a double indicator.

B Correct. The subject is *one group of stars*. The main noun is *group*, which is a collective noun. Collective nouns are considered singular, so you need the singular verb *was*.

C Incorrect. The word *especially* is spelled correctly in the passage.

D Incorrect. This sentence contains a usage mistake.

Question 6 (page 143)

Adjective/Adverb

A Incorrect. The writer is trying to say *we are*, so the correct word is the contraction *we're*.

B Incorrect. The comma after *away* is needed because the phrase that follows is a participial phrase.

C Correct. The sky at the center is being compared to the sky in other places, so a comparative adjective needs to be used. The comparative form of the word *dark* is *darker*.

D Incorrect. A comparison is being made, so *than* is the correct word.

Question 7 (page 144)

Awkward Sentence

A Incorrect. This answer choice is still awkward, and it's also a run-on sentence, two complete sentences separated by only a comma.

B Correct. This answer choice is a clear, complete sentence.

C Incorrect. This answer choice contains a fragment (*Because the air in this climate contains little moisture*).

D Incorrect. This answer choice is awkward, and it's inaccurate. It suggests that the night sky is what does the distorting.

Question 8 (page 144)

Quotation Marks

A Incorrect. The phrase is *our observatory*. A possessive pronoun is needed, so *our* is the correct word, not *are*.

B Incorrect. Steve has been talking to the group in the present tense. It wouldn't make sense to suddenly shift to past tense.

C Correct. This is the end of the words said by staff member Steve. Quotation marks should be used to close the quote.

D Incorrect. There is a punctuation mistake in this sentence. Quotation marks are missing.

Question 9 (page 144)

Indefinite Reference

A Incorrect. *We* is still a pronoun. It does not clarify whom the sentence is about. Also, *we* is in the first person. The author has not been writing in the first person.

B Incorrect. It doesn't make sense that the volunteers would be doing the peering. Furthermore, if that noun were used, the sentence would become redundant.

C Incorrect. Steve isn't going to aid himself.

D Correct. This is the answer that makes sense based on the context of the paragraph and the rest of the story. Members of the astronomy club would be the ones peering through the telescopes since they were the ones on the field trip.

Question 10 (page 144)

Extraneous Sentence

A Incorrect. This is the opening sentence of the last paragraph, and it states the paragraph's main idea.

B Incorrect. It wouldn't make sense to describe what the students did and then write *then came the best part of the star party*.

C Correct. This sentence does not fit in the logical progression of the rest of the paragraph.

D Incorrect. The students wouldn't have gone back to their lodging before they looked through the telescopes.

"Living with the Chimps"

Question 11 (page 147)

Parallelism

A Correct. This is a clear, complete sentence, and the ideas are expressed in a parallel way.

B Incorrect. This answer choice includes a sentence fragment (*To also write about the animals*).

C Incorrect. This answer choice is a run-on sentence because it is two complete sentences separated by only a comma.

D Incorrect. The ideas in the original sentence are not expressed in a parallel way. The phrases *living with* and *to write about* need to be parallel.

Question 12 (page 147)

Word Usage

A Incorrect. The noun *world* is singular, so the possessive is formed by adding -*'s*.

B Incorrect. The comma is used to separate the relative clause from the main clause.

C Correct. The writer is making a comparison, so *than* is the correct word to use.

D Incorrect. There is a usage error in this sentence.

Question 13 (page 147)

Sequence/Progression

A Correct. Sentence 7 starts with the words *in those days*. Sentence 8 needs to come first so that the reader knows what days the writer is referring to.

B Incorrect. Sentence 11 can't be deleted because then readers wouldn't know who Leakey is when he is mentioned in sentence 12.

C Incorrect. The writer needs to tell readers who Leakey is before telling that he hired Goodall to serve as his assistant.

D Incorrect. Sentence 12 can't be moved. It should follow sentence 11 since they both talk about Goodall's involvement with Leakey.

Question 14 (page 147)

Run-on Sentence

A Incorrect. This answer choice contains a fragment (*And soon realized that she had found her life's work*).

B Incorrect. This answer choice contains a fragment (*Excited by what she experienced and learned on her trip*).

C Correct. This answer choice is a clear, complete sentence.

D Incorrect. The sentence in the passage is a run-on because it is two complete sentences separated by only a comma.

Question 15 (page 147)

Apostrophe

A Incorrect. The passage is in the past tense, so there is no reason to shift tenses in this sentence.

B Correct. This sentence refers to many chimpanzees, not just one. The apostrophe should follow the *s*.

C Incorrect. The plural form of *life* is formed by changing the *f* to a *v* and then adding -*s*. The word is spelled correctly in the passage.

D Incorrect. There is a punctuation mistake in this sentence.

Question 16 (page 147)

Fragment

A Incorrect. This answer choice is awkward and inaccurate. It suggests that the primates were recording information.

B Incorrect. This answer choice is a run-on because it is two complete sentences separated by only a comma.

C Correct. This answer choice is a clear, complete sentence.

D Incorrect. Sentences 16 and 17 should be combined because sentence 17 is a fragment.

Question 17 (page 148)

Supporting Sentence

A Incorrect. This is an opinion that doesn't belong in this type of paper.

B Incorrect. This statement repeats what was already said in sentence 19.

C Incorrect. This paragraph is about what Goodall learned about the chimps. It doesn't really matter that tools can be made from many materials.

D Correct. This sentence supports sentence 19 because it tells an effect of Goodall's discoveries.

Question 18 (page 148)

Capitalization

A Incorrect. If you insert *it was* after *jungle*, you will create a run-on.

B Incorrect. There is no reason to insert a comma before the prepositional phrase in this sentence.

C Correct. Cambridge University is the name of a specific university, so it is a proper noun that must be capitalized.

D Incorrect. There is a capitalization mistake in this sentence.

Question 19 (page 148)

Semicolon

A   Incorrect. The Jane Goodall Institute is the name of a specific institute, so it is a proper noun and must be capitalized.

B   Correct. The sentence in the passage is a run-on because it is two complete sentences separated by only a comma. One way to correct a run-on is to put a semicolon between the two sentences.

C   Incorrect. The word *provide* ends in a silent *-e*. When a word ends in a silent *-e*, you drop the *-e* before adding *-ing*.

D   Incorrect. There is a punctuation mistake in this sentence.

Question 20 (page 148)

Make No Change

A   Incorrect. The word *familiar* is spelled correctly in the passage.

B   Incorrect. The correct homonym is used in the passage. The writer is referring to a place, so *there* is correct. The word *their* is used to show ownership.

C   Incorrect. Changing *and* to *it is* would create a run-on.

D   Correct. This sentence does not need to be changed.

DISCARD